Discourses on
Ethics and Business

Published in conjunction with
The Ethics Resource Center

Discourses on
Ethics and Business

Jack N. Behrman
University of North Carolina

Oelgeschlager, Gunn & Hain, Inc.
Publishers
1278 Massachusetts Ave., Harvard Square, Cambridge, MA 02138

International Standard Book Number: 0-89946-064-x

Library of Congress Catalog Card Number:80-23626

Printed in West Germany

Library of Congress Cataloging in Publication Data

Behrman, Jack N
  Ethics and Business.

  1. Business ethics—Addresses, essays, lectures.
2. Industry—Social aspects—Addresses, essays, lectures. I. Title.
HF5387.B43   174'.4   80-23626
ISBN 0-89946-064-x

To the memories of Governor Luther H. Hodges, who, as Secretary of Commerce, guided me, and Dr. C. K. Brown, who, as my professor at Davidson College, started me along this road.

Contents

Preface

These discourses are a result of several years of lectures and dialogues with managers in a variety of executive development programs, and of presentations before business audiences on social changes affecting the role of business.

The purpose of publishing them is to respond to requests that they be made available to other groups for discussion. Some of the presentations were taped and have been edited only slightly; they are therefore somewhat loose, and sometimes detour from the main topic to pursue concerns of the group. The purpose, then as now, is to involve the participants in an examination of the issues. It is *not* to provide solutions, which in any case change in their specifics from case to case. The reader may wish that firm answers were given, but those would depend on the writer's ethical values, whereas the purpose is for the reader to discover and apply his own values.

The subjects covered have been chosen to probe the fundamental ethical content of business activities. The first five chapters are sequential. The following five can be taken up in any order. The chapters do not purport to treat even the major subjects on which corporate or managerial responsibility should be exercised. Neither do they constitute a text or a thesis in any sense. They are best suited to small, informal dialogues and could readily be complemented by a variety of other topics, such as "management and labor," "environmental concerns," or "technology and economic progress." Selected readings are provided to add other views on the subjects included in the book.

Although each of the subjects presented lends itself to scholarly research and analysis, no attempt is made here to provide justification for the statements nor to appeal to authority for support. Each of the statements made, however, is in my view defensible. The sources of ideas and arguments are too numerous to cite; many are virtually untraceable, as they have been gathered over several years in a long learning process.

In addition, although some of the views are couched in a somewhat contentious mode, no attempt is made to be provocative merely for the sake of disturbing the reader. The issues themselves are likely to be abrasive, even with tender handling. The objective is to raise issues which are confronting business and which require a serious response from managers both individually and collectively.

Underlying the several discourses is the belief and argument that U.S. business—as a system—has departed significantly from the characteristics of the system explained by Adam Smith in 1776 and later called "capitalism," and that these changes have moved us away from the ethical justifications for that particular system. We are searching for new justifications as a consequence. In order for our institutions and ourselves to remain free, we must return to some basic ethical concepts. These ethical concepts relate to the justification for our business system, sometimes called the "private enterprise system," and the implications of business decisions for social and economic goals, sometimes called the "social contract." For the system to be acceptable, the *justifications* must be rooted in social values. And for the activities and impact of business to be acceptable to society, the *implications*—impacts, roles, and duties— must occur or be carried out with the individual values of honesty, truthfulness, mutual trust, responsibility, and the rest. Chapters 1 through 4 are concerned primarily with *justification* and the changes rung in the system; the remainder are primarily concerned with the *implications* for responsibility of business and its managers.

The fact that these issues are critical is underscored by the statement by Harvard Business School students that the role of managers as treated in their curriculum appeared as "a-ethical," and by the results of a survey (reported in *Business Week*, January 31, 1977, p. 107) in which the executives of two companies responded anonymously that personal ethics were under pressure of compromise by business demands. Seventy percent of Uniroyal managers reported feeling these pressures; at Pitney-Bowes' the figure was 59 percent. Though most replied that they personally would not, for example, sell offstandard or dangerous products, they believed that others in the company would. They also believed that in all companies "the individual is expendable." On a more positive note, most managers asserted that they would like "to believe their particular job can be done with a high degree of ethics. It is up to corporate management to confirm this belief."

The specific responses required of business to maintain freedom are not easy to set forth, but the fundamental ethical values are readily recognizable. Without a rejuvenated pursuit of those values, we will find ourselves moving in a direction which many of us would abhor and reject.

If these discourses stimulate careful thought and constructive action by managers to regain an accepted central role in the improvement of the life of peoples seeking to remain free, they will have achieved their purpose.

Jack N. Behrman
Chapel Hill, N.C.

Chapter 1

Ethical Values Underlying
Capitalism

To give you an idea of what the first few sessions are about, I'd like
to quote A. A. Berle, who was one of the close observers of American
capitalism in the 1930s and 1940s:

> The really great corporation management must consciously take account
> of philosophical considerations. They must consider the kind of com-
> munity in which they have faith and which they will serve and which they
> intend to help construct and maintain. In a word, they must consider at
> least in its elementary phases the ancient problems of the good life and
> how their operations in the community can be adapted to affording or
> fostering it.

I don't think I can find a better way of expressing the ethical problem which faces American management today. American management is seen as destroying some of the basic values in our society,
and at the same time it is held responsible for creating the good life,
or for improving the quality of life. Business is very much involved
in the total economy. It affects nearly all our activities in the society.
Questions are being raised about whether business is operating in
ways that are good for the society and about what role business
should play in it. These questions were answered two centuries ago.

I want us to consider the origins of capitalism and some of the ways it has changed in America. These three subjects—the values underlying capitalism, its institutions, and modifications in its operation—will be examined in the first three discourses. In the third, we will examine why we've gone so far off the path described by Adam Smith in 1776, and what is causing our present malaise, as reflected in the lack of confidence in both business and government institutions.

The later chapters go into some of the reasons why we're having so much difficulty correcting the problems and why so much of our attention is focused on government, rather than business, solving our problems. As you read through the description of the early concepts of capitalism, you will notice that the government's role was small. We have shifted responsibilities over the past couple of hundred years, and that has annoyed business—in some sense, properly so. But that's the story of the development of capitalism—the increasing encroachment of government on the kinds of decisions that business was supposed to make.

Now, however, let's turn to the role of values in our economic and business system—looking first at values themselves: their types, origins, and roles in our economic system and business behavior.

One cannot understand *any* social system or *any* public policy without first understanding the values that underlie that system or its goals—the value goals for which the system was designed or by which it is justified. One of the major conflicts confronting businesses (or managers) arises when the values underlying their business or management goals differ from those of the socioeconomic system.

For a *system* to be accepted, it must be seen as "good." And as soon as we say the word "good," we have gone beyond the realm of managerial efficiency and pursuit of quantifiable goals and entered the world of values—that is, the concepts of what is a "good life," or the desired "quality of life," or happiness.

Very few participants in our social system, or its social institutions, really understand the values that underlay the system of capitalism as it was justified 200 years ago, and which we pay lip service to today. Why not? Why don't we stop to think about the values within which we are rooted?

We either forget the underlying values *or* we have conflicting objectives that are based on other values. We have not kept our original values. Why not? For one thing, problems don't always come up in a fashion permitting us to say "this is good and this is bad." All sorts of pressures are involved—personalities, who you know, elections, and so on. And these things get in the way of neatly relying on basic values.

Values underlie everything, however. They underlie your reason for joining this discussion: you, or someone else, think it is a "good thing" for you to participate in executive development, and that "good thing" is related to something else that someone thinks is "good."

TYPES OF VALUES

Let's get down to fundamentals. Where do we get values, and how were they put into the Capitalist system, and then what happened to them?

There are basically two types of values: ethical and pragmatic. Ethical values are often seen as universal, and pragmatic ones as relative. We often reverse this characterization, however, making ethical values relative to different cultures and situations (situational ethics). In fact, *ethical* values can be viewed as either "universal" or "relative," with the value of honesty and truthfulness derived from (relative to) the value of having an open democracy or an effective student–teacher relation, which requires truthfulness and honest communication. Universal ethical values would be those that are inborn or a part of human nature—wisdom, courage, reverence, kindness, gratitude—and that distinguish human beings from "lower" forms of life.

Frequently, we assert that some action is valuable because it works, and that is the pragmatic value. For example, President Kennedy was said to be a pragmatic president in the sense that he looked for what worked. Pragmatic efficiency may be valuable, but it is distinct from ethical values—although business often seems to elevate efficiency to an independent (ethical) value as "good" of itself. This is done in order to sidestep the conflict between an action that is seen as pragmatically valuable ("we made a profit, didn't we?") and more universal values such as honesty and responsibility. This sidestepping is also an excuse at times to subvert personal ethics in favor of company goals, under the argument that personal values are inappropriate as standards for corporate decisions.

These concepts are important in assessing a business system: if the goal is to produce a higher standard of living, does it make any difference *how* you do it? If I can demonstrate to you that Communist *methods* will produce economic growth more efficiently, does that mean they should be adopted? Does the *end* now appear so good? You can't divorce ends from means, and yet we do so much of the time. Brazil now has one of the highest standards of living in Latin America; it has adopted certain repressive means—for the purpose of achieving a higher standard of living. Its motto is "Order and Progress," but nothing is said of "equality, liberty, and fraternity." And President Carter has said, in effect: "You shouldn't do it that way—not the right means to a good end! You should extend human rights to all." At the same time American business is helping Brazil more than any foreign government is. We made tradeoffs among our goals. Which values are we pursuing?[a]

ORIGINS OF VALUES

Where did we get our ethical values? Where did we get our ideas of "good"? I don't know of any society—and I've studied a good many of them now, since I've been teaching a course on management styles around the world—that doesn't have a set of religious beliefs that are the basic source of many of its values. It's not the only source of values, but it is a basic source. The religious beliefs obviously are different among societies in actual practice when it comes to what is seen as "good." For example, President Khadaffi of Libya believes that what the *Koran* commands is in fact "good," down to the precise punishment for theft, which includes cutting off the thief's right hand in a public square. (Incidentally, the right hand is cut off, instead of the left, because it's the hand that goes into the food bowl. The left hand is unclean: it's the one you clean your bottom with, and thus you may not use it to dip into the bowl. Therefore, you may not eat with anyone else—i.e., you are ostracized—if you have no right hand. This is a rather harsh and continuing punishment, but it is matched to the values of the religious system.)

Where do religious values come from? More precisely, where do we *believe* that religious values come from? Where do they come from in the Koran? Mohammad said Allah dictated them! Many believe that the books of the Bible were inspired by God. What does Buddha say about his teachings? That they were revealed. Religious roots are said to come from God, Himself. If, in fact, religious values all over the world are believed to come from God, one would suppose that they should not be casually overlooked. Yet we do overlook them!

a. The addendum to this chapter raises this issue for U.S. relations with the developing countries.

Perhaps because we don't believe they came from God. The root is there, nevertheless, and it is the strongest possible root to our values.

Obviously, if we don't like what is in the Bible or the Koran or in Buddha's teachings, we will find ways to argue about them. Controversy arises within and between most religious groups—between Protestants and Catholics and Jews it is common; certain Muslim and Buddhist sects are literally fighting among themselves. We're not always sure that we "like" the values that come from our religions, so we alter them in practice.

People sometimes hold values simply because they have adopted a whole set of beliefs, not knowing even where they came from. Such beliefs are held tenaciously, in part because the holder does not know how to derive others. Thus, if you say that you *believe* something, it is exceedingly difficult for anyone to cause you to give up that belief. There may be no rational root to your belief—simply affirmation. If you do get pushed in an argument back through your process of reasoning, you will frequently find that the place where you stop is the point where your beliefs are challenged. If someone argues with you, at some point you'll say, "I'm sorry; I just believe . . .," and that finishes it.

Such beliefs have a complex set of origins, often traditional, sometimes religious, or rational. They have to do with the teachings of one's mother and father, with school experiences, visits to grandparents, any number of things. They are modifications of our thinking arising from our environment and our teachers, and they are different all over the world.

There's another basic origin of values which can be called intellectual or metaphysical. We find no physical or sentient basis for these values: they are arrived at by rational thought. This intellectual root says, in effect: "I figured it out! This is the best thing to do." The group known as the Humanists search intellectually for their values; they consider that they've figured out the best (ethical) system for man. By intellectual activity, they have come up with a system which they consider to be ethically the best. They do not ask where they got this intelligence or how they figured it out, necessarily; they simply believe in the power of rationality.

I will not rank the validity of these roots. Both are valid in terms of the creation of the ethical system within which we operate, and in fact they are often mixed.[b] The values underlying Capitalism are certainly both religious and intellectual.

b. Some writers wish to distinguish these two roots by designating religious values as "moral" and intellectual values as "ethical," but they do not have widespread support for this distinction, and efforts to illustrate the differences

UNDERLYING VALUES
OF CAPITALISM

Two basic values form the ethical foundations of Capitalism: *individualism* and *utilitarianism*. Individualism says that the individual is the most important entity in society. It isn't the state or anyone in government, but the individual who should be considered paramount. Notice the word *should*: as soon as we say it, where are we? Back into values again. Back to assumptions about what is good.

Where does the idea of the individual as the prime entity come from? It doesn't exist all over the world. It seems to me that in fact there aren't more than three or four nations left which share this particular belief—the Anglo-Saxon societies of the U.S., the U.K., Canada, and Australia, maybe, with some variations in the European countries.

Where does the idea come from? What is the basic justification for the idea that the individual should be paramount? It has both religious and intellectual roots. The religious root goes all the way back to Genesis—further, in fact, because Genesis was written after the beliefs came into being. Genesis, says that "man was created in God's image." It doesn't say the family was created in God's image. It doesn't say the society was created in God's image. It doesn't say the Israelites were created in God's image. It says that "man was created in God's image." And the purpose of man is to do what? To glorify God! Which means to become one with God, to achieve oneness with God—as Christ later said, "be ye perfect, even as your Father in Heaven is perfect."

That momentous assertion is one of the origins of the concept of individualism in our belief system: the individual is to be the entity we are concerned with. The *individual* is to evolve until he (or she) reaches God's perfection. (Whether *all* is to be accomplished here on earth or, even if so, through one or several incarnations distinguishes a lot of belief systems.) This belief was basic to the Protestant Reformation—a necessary foundation, according to many, for the building of Capitalism.

---

often fall into the trap that "ethical" values become relativistic (getting their justification from some *other* asserted value), leaving "moral" values to be universal—which, of course, they are not, because there is no universal religion. They can be universal if there is, in fact, only one God (or Ultimate Reality) and He has revealed His Truth in some manner.

In Japan, where ancestors are the only gods, morals are what is codified into law, and ethical behavior comes from ancestral instruction passed down in the culture.

Let's look at it: If any man can control you, your chances for perfection are no better than his. For each individual to achieve *his* image in God, to achieve *his* perfection according to *his* ability, he must be free. This belief prompted the Protestant reformers to withdraw from the Catholic Church in order to let *every* man speak directly with God, rather than go through the Catholic hierarchy. The belief in individualism has widespread implications—for social, as well as religious, institutions. Capitalism, for example, was justified at the outset as the economic system that permitted man to achieve his creative excellence as an individual. You don't depend on anybody else to do it; it is up to you!

Why all Christian systems didn't develop the same kind of capitalism is a story we won't go into in detail. French Capitalism is not British Capitalism, German Capitalism is not French Capitalism, Italian Capitalism is like neither one of them, and American Capitalism has its own unique structure. One of the reasons for such differences is the fact that the religious root of individualism was mixed with a philosophical root leading to democracy in the political arena—a philosophical justification for removal of strong or centralized government in favor of greater participation by the governed. The philosophical root was expressed in our own Declaration of Independence, building on the philosophies of John Locke and David Hume. These English philosophers were not wholly accepted on the European Continent. Catholicism also held greater sway there than in England or America. It is from combining the political and economic systems based on individualism that we get the name "democratic capitalism," which does *not* describe the method of decision-making in Capitalism, but the political system under which it operates.

The other basic value, utilitarianism, arises from a philosophy (and a psychology) that says that man and woman are pleasure–seeking animals. They seek pleasure over pain, hedonistically, and avoid pain whenever they can. They seek to minimize pain and maximize pleasure. This is an empirical observation of the nature of the individual's drives, leading to the intellectual conclusion that, since he or she is designed this way, this is the way he or she *ought* to be.

The utilitarian philosophers recognized that pleasure could be sought in virtually any way. They were quite clear to say that pushpin, which was a game of the day similar to checkers, is as good as poetry in terms of delivering pleasure. Some people like checkers and other people like poetry! (Though John Stuart Mill did argue that there was a qualitative hierarchy among pleasures, making some "better" or "higher" than others.) The pursuit of pleasure also involves individualism. *You* decide what is pleasurable to you; nobody else! If I tell you (when you want to go to a movie), "you ought to get pleasure out of a Picasso, and I want you to go to the exhibit with me", I may be interfering in your individual pursuit of pleasure. You are likely to respond, "I don't like Picasso. I couldn't care less about his painting. I want to go to the movie." Hedonism says, "Go!"

The hedonist philosophers concluded that maximization of pleasure is what society should be all about. (Notice "should be," again!) But a fundamental question arises about how to make sure that the *society* achieves maximum pleasure when *individuals* are seeking their own pleasures. Supposedly, you can add up individual pleasures and get a better society. But suppose I sum the pleasures. Is there any way I can be sure that everybody is *better off* because everybody is pleased? In other words, does the sum of individual pleasures actually equal the total social pleasure? Not if some people get pleasure out of inflicting pain on others. The evidence that we do is discrimination—of any sort whatsoever—the reluctance to let all individuals have equal opportunity. We *must* get pleasure out of that, since we do it so often. We apparently have some feeling or rational view that discrimination is good for us, and that won't work for society as a whole.

Bentham, the father of hedonistic calculus, asserted that the system should provide "the greatest good for the greatest number." Now that is fine, but it sets *two* maximums. You mathematicians, how do you achieve *two* maximums simultaneously? Is it possible? Or is one a constraint? How can we calculate the pleasure of the greatest number?; and notice that we have not subtracted the pain of the least number. If we are going to design a society for the majority, and calculate total pleasure/pain, we have to know *how painful* it is to the minority. We get trapped in a myriad of problems. Besides, what is the greatest number? 800 million in China—at a living standard of $100 per capita a year. Compare that to the U.S., with 220 million at a per capita income of $10,000. Which is better? Since we can't compare the pleasure of the two groups, Bentnam's maxim isn't really helpful. It doesn't solve the problem of how to *direct* or constrain the actions of individuals. Hedonism, nevertheless, is one of the roots of Capitalism.

The other roots do lead to constraints on the individual. The philosophical root of individualism led to constraints, because no individual was supposed to be free to deny the freedom of others. Freedom was seen as individual but also indivisible—if anyone lost his freedom, others were threatened. Therefore, individualism also required social responsibility to maintain the system for the benefit of all.

Social responsibility is part of the Judeo-Christian tradition. Calvin wanted to set up a Christian society in Geneva, putting into effect the principles of the Old Testament, including the work ethic and the strictures of the Proverbs. Individuals were supposed to exert themselves, not just to be creative but to fulfill the responsibility of stewardship. Individuals were to seek gain, to be rich, but to use it for the benefit of the society. The Old Testament states clearly that, if you are *good*, your reward will be riches on earth. Calvin concluded that a good society would be wealthy. Individuals would be rich, but, according to Calvin, they were not supposed to enjoy it. That constraint is still deep within our beliefs about *how* we should to respond to the accumulation of material goods.

We blended religious individualism with hedonism, however, and that means we're supposed to enjoy! We set up a system to maximize individual pleasures because that's what people are striving for. In the process, our concepts of hedonism changed. We began to define pleasure as the pursuit of *material* pleasures—and further excluding pleasures that do not have a *price*. Pleasures could include listening to a lecture or to poetry or whatever, but if *free*, they did not represent *economic* (material) gains. Since the system is supposed to produce gains (growth), we have focused our attention on material (marketable) goods and services. Individual pursuit of the joy of fishing is not in the economic system—unless it is paid for directly. If you pay $200 to go floating down a river, fishing off the side of a boat, that pleasure has a monetary value, and the economy is said to be better off by the amount of the *payment* (not the pleasure). But, if you go off with your fishing rod and sit by a pond and contemplate the infinite, that doesn't count in the system of economic pleasure as we have defined it. We have begun, by the *way* in which we measure pleasures, to *restrict* what the system is about. The goal becomes *material* growth and the efficient pursuit of that growth— in other words, hedonism and pragmatism. We have thus defined the system as pleasure-oriented by defining the opportunity to exercise individual creative abilities.

The implications of this view are serious. We have chosen to rely on *quantitative* measures for our goals rather than the more complex and indefinite qualitative measures which are used in value trade-offs. We can and do, at times, act as though one value is greater than another—loyalty over truth, for example—, but the values shift in relation to one another. Since it is difficult to pin these values down, leaving bases for decision-making indefinite, we have substituted quantitatively measured targets. But quantitative measures should be applied to means, determining their efficiency or effectiveness—not to ends. When ends are measured quantitatively, responsibility is diminished. We will pick up this issue again in Chapter 10.

I urge you to consider the ethical roots carefully. If you have agreed with me so far, then you have to watch out, because (as you were told long ago in your college days) if you grant somebody his assumptions, unless he's a fool, he wins the argument. You might ask, Wasn't our economy built on individualism? Yes, both our Declaration of Independence and Constitution reflect the concept of individualism, and our leaders and builders acted the part. The frontier movement was an expression of the desire of the individual not to be controlled, or not to be interfered with in his individual pursuits, be they pleasurable or otherwise. As Daniel Boone said, "I've got to move on 'cause my neighbor's now only 30 miles away." This was merely his expression of an individual drive that was permissible in the early, frontier days. Had we been settled by people who did not have such a concept of individualism, we would have a quite different society today. (The society which existed here before the settlers came, the Indian society, was *not* an individualistic society.) The frontier, in offering an opportunity for the expression of individualism, was basic to the formation of American Capitalism and Democracy—as compared to the Italian, German or French systems. We still retain some of that "damned the hind-most" individualism of the frontier. The frontier had another characteristic that arose from being so close to starvation in a survival society— the sense of community and sharing and helping the afflicted. In many of the frontier communities that sense arose from traditional religious beliefs—once again, a source of values.

I'd like also to suggest that you read carefully the piece by Charles Malik that follows, for it is an excellent statement of the problems arising from turning material means into goals and forgetting or subverting ethical values. Though it was written in 1965, its message is still quite current. Dr. Malik represented Lebanon as Ambassador to the U.S., and subsequently served as President of the U.N. General Assembly, from 1958 to 1959; later he was Distinguished Professor of Philosophy at the American University of Beirut.

* * *

ADDENDUM: "WHAT SHALL IT
PROFIT A MAN. . . ?"–
by Charles H. Malik*

A Conspicuous Absence of Proof

Scanning the free arena of history, I find no evidence that the communist and communizing countries are faring better than the capitalist and capitalizing ones. The latter appear to be stronger, happier, more prosperous, more energetic, and the subjects of the envy of the former. They are tackling their many economic and social problems with increasing wisdom and success, and without sacrificing their essential freedom. There is far greater nostalgia for freedom in the realm of communism and dictatorship than there is yearning for communism and dictatorship in the realm of freedom. The Berlin wall is dramatic proof of that, and there are many other walls of a different nature that can also be adduced as proofs. Moreover, there has been some experimentation with freedom and individual incentive in the communist economies. I find the problems of these economies at least as formidable as those of free ones. And in the world of the emerging countries themselves, every one that has not sacrificed its freedom upon the altar of socialism and dictatorship is happier, healthier, and more prosperous than those who have. It is a myth, therefore, a dogmatic and doctrinaire myth, to hold that the best the underdeveloped countries can look forward to is some socializing, communizing, and dictatorializing regime. At least it is an unproven proposition.

Is Development the Preeminent Good?

But what if it were founded on solid evidence? What if socialism, communism, and dictatorship were indeed prerequisites to development? One has then to ask whether economic development is worth the purchase price, if that price is not merely the destruction of ossified social and cultural conditions, but also the weakening of cherished free values. Is development the highest value, and are all other values subsidiary, left to scramble for position as best they can underneath the preeminent good? To be human, to experience that

*Appreciation is due the Conference Board for permission to reprint this talk given during the Second International Industrial Conference, San Francisco, California, September 13-17, 1965, co-sponsored with the Stanford Research Institute.

inner joy which only the free know, to trust your reason, to be unafraid, to seek the truth wherever you may find it, to discuss even the absurd, to be interested in the affairs of your government in such a way as to effect a difference in its tone and its direction, to worship God as your conscience dictates—are all these values of freedom unimportant unless they serve the nation or help to increase its gross national product?

There are many who believe that development is the invariable and that all other things fluctuate; and if any value cannot find a place for itself in the development-oriented society, then so much the worse for it. These pontiffs of development reveal that in their scale of values, freedom does not come first. If this is not the case, then let them dare say so—and act on what they say. Let them behave, theoretically and practically, so as to convince us that they regard nondevelopmental values as more important, and that in the event of an irreconcilable conflict, they would cast aside development to preserve freedom. Let them reaffirm what they know or should know: that all the full stomachs, all the high standards of living, all the development in the world, cannot by themselves make one man honest, or magnanimous, or grand, or sincere, or pure, or forgiving, or humble, or loving, or happy, or self-sacrificing.

It is worthwhile pointing out that those who reject freedom for development really run the risk of losing both. Development depends, both positively and negatively, on its ends and purposes. Positively, because the end always determines the means to be taken to achieve it. And negatively, because if the spirit you are developing is warlike and aggressive, the rest of the world is not going to sit idly by. If the kind of person your civilization is producing is obnoxious, incongruous, arrogant, contradicting, nihilistic, and full of hatred, the rest of the world is going to do something about it. It all depends on the kind of spirit your development generates. Surely everybody has every right to develop himself, but always within the strict limits of consideration for others. China cannot go on developing itself in a manner repugnant to others, including Russia; sooner or later this disapproval is going to make itself felt. And there are many little Chinas whose development is under the daily scrutiny of the rest of the world. When the time of reckoning comes, many a development can only end in setting back its people hundreds of years.

The Price Is Spiritual Poverty

It is thus the tragedy of the underdeveloped world that many of its leaders promise their peoples material abundance, and either cannot deliver or can only do so at the price of a spiritual poverty which threatens the stability of the material gains themselves. In many of these countries freedom, in every sense of the term, especially in the personal, spiritual sense, is being overcome by unfreedom. The mind is becoming absolutely terrorized against standing up for man and truth, while the intellectual classes—the teachers, students, thinkers, and poets—grow estranged from the concepts of a free society.

Much of the fault belongs to the West. The West which has aroused and awakened the desires of these peoples and fed them false and extravagant hopes, and then, when hopes and desires were unful-filled, said: "Well, the only thing is to keep the lid down, and prevent the caldrom from boiling over, by strong and dictatorial government." The West which has spoken about man and freedom in muffled voices, and which has conceded to the foes of freedom by arguing, in effect, that the only difference between them and it is that whereas they want progress by revolution and force, the West wants it by evo-lution and peace. This is pernicious nonsense, for the real difference is not in the method of reaching the end, but in the character of the end itself—the kind of man and spirit and civilization that will then emerge.

The tragedy of the industrialized world is that its thinkers no longer believe and project its ultimate values—I mean, believe in the human person, in the ultimacy of man and his freedom, in the crea-tive originality of the mind and sprit, in objective truth, in the ability of the mind to grasp it, in the potency of love, and in the reality of God. They try to explain these values away; in fact, they are ashamed of them, or they preach their relativity, either to special cultures or to special epochs. They come to the underdeveloped peoples conceal-ing from them their ultimate values? And why? Because they no longer know them! They thus deceive the underdeveloped by re-vealing to them only the superficial, the external, the merest crumbs of existence. Nothing is more tragic than the sight of a man having everything, and yet, in approaching the desperately needy, not giving of what he has, either because he does not really know what he has or because he no longer believes in it.

It is a question of faith in the values of freedom. This is a most serious matter. If the leaders of the developed world are ashamed of their system and its values, if they believe that these values are good for their own people but not for all men, if their thinkers keep on dinning into the ears of the world the unproved proposition that their system is not good enough for the underdeveloped countries, if capitalism continues to be a term of reproach, if free enterprise is treated with contempt by the people of Asia and Africa, if capitalism and free enterprise are not going to be rehabilitated morally, if the idea of "development at any price" is accepted without question— if this state of affairs continues to reign, I believe that the West is already licked, and awaits only the final *coup de grace*. I am not thinking of the crude, cutthroat, individualistic capitalism of the 19th century; I am thinking of the mature and socially responsible system of today. I am thinking of the ultimate values of freedom which lie behind this system, values which have been preserved through and despite the maturation of this system, values which have made possible, not only the system itself, but the dearest possessions of western civilization.

This is not a question of professors or of propaganda. It is a question of the highest statesmanship, one that has been thoroughly aroused to the terrible crisis of the age. The recent drift must be brought to an end. Shame, apology, hesitation, uncertainty, the sense of inferiority and guilt, all this must be ruthlessly brushed aside. Man, his freedom and spirit, must be reinstated in their place. The greatest values of the western heritage must be rediscovered and reaffirmed, and all the alien values must never be allowed to obscure or overwhelm them. There is no meaning to this moment of history save to rise resolutely to this challenge.

Three Stages of Association

It is only by striving to meet this challenge that the Western nations can fashion meaningful relations with the underdeveloped world. The association of developed and less developed historically has covered three stages. The first stage is colonial domination, but since the spirit cannot stand domination indefinitely, a rebellion ensues. This leads to the second stage, to which I apply the term "monadic independence." Here the detached colony wishes to be left all alone. But it soon discovers that it needs the developed world, and so it seeks to enter into new creative relations with it, this time on the basis of equality and mutual respect. The first stage—association between unequals—is false, because the stronger tends to dominate and exploit the weaker. The second stage—dissociation into monadic equals—is abstract, because the weaker desperately needs the stronger. The third stage—reassociation between equals—is stable, provided the limits of equality are carefully discriminated. Such then is the law of development in the relations of the more- to the less-developed countries of the world.

The first two stages are mostly behind us: colonialism has gone, but so has monadic independence. Our era is the third stage in which new associations are developed between equals. But equality here cannot possibly be absolute: it can only be sovereign and moral equality. It is mutual respect between the otherwise unequal. For generations and perhaps centuries to come, new creative associations are going to be sought between the countries of Asia, Africa, the Middle East, and Latin America, on the one hand, and the more developed countries, on the other.

They Only Ask to Belong

The most important principle of the new association is to make the underdeveloped countries feel in truth that they belong. It is not a matter of giving, nor a matter of taking, nor even a matter of giving and taking; it is a matter of belonging. The developing countries must feel that they belong to humanity, that they have a part, indeed an honorable and important part, to play in the drama of being. As soon as man suspects that something of transcendent importance is going on somewhere, which he cannot appreciate or understand or take part in or enact himself, from which he is debarred in principle, the spirit is soured at the core. Man must feel that he belongs. This is a task that will tax the powers of the highest statesmanship, the highest thought, and the deepest spirit. But it is a task that must and can be accomplished.

The evil of the colonial system is not so much its exploitation as its moral treatment of peoples as inferior, as not belonging. The oppressed soon internalize this feeling so that they believe their masters and begin to look upon themselves as not belonging. This is all so false, so untrue. Man essentially belongs. The underdeveloped peoples would put up with any suffering, any inequality, any task assigned to them, if only they believed that they belonged. Part of the genius of communism is precisely its ability to include them, to banish their feeling of estrangement.

In the spirit of including him, of giving him the sense of belonging, of taking him into communion, you can turn to underdeveloped man and address him as follows, and, with a twinkle in his eye, he will understand you perfectly, without the slightest resentment:

> You have every right to be independent and every right to develop your-self in freedom. But you must acknowledge that you are not really independent of others and you cannot develop yourself alone. The more fortunate peoples—more fortunate physically, naturally, scientifically, culturally, spiritually—are themselves the bearers of history, destiny, and creativity. You are a very nice fellow and all that, but ultimate responsibility before time and eternity resides more in the developed nations than

in you. You resent the phrase 'the sacred trust of civilization' being applied to you, and of course if the developed nations used this phrase with a sense of pride and superiority, they would be wrong, and some day they would suffer retribution for it. But it is a fact that you do constitute a 'sacred trust' for these peoples. Nothing is more obvious than that you cannot be independent of Europe, Russia, and America, nor can you develop yourself without them. This raises tremendous issues of responsibility both for you and for them. For them, because they must pray that they be worthy of the wonderful blessings of which they are the custodians. And for you, because there are limits to how much you can envy them, or hate them, or wish them ill, or play them off against each other.

The heart of man craves rest and peace even more than motion and development—the rest and peace of fellowship. In fact, all development is in order to land him ultimately in that. Imagine then perfect love, perfect trust, perfect power, perfect fellowship, perfect understanding, perfect warmth of intimacy and belonging, and you have already entered into life eternal. I assure you man does not want more than that. Give him that, and he does not mind death itself. Only the lonely fear death, but not the beloved. When you insist on development and progress, it is presumably because you cannot assure him of love and fellowship and forgiveness. Man says: if only I am understood, if only I am trusted, if only I have a friend, if only I am given a chance, if only I have a lover, if only I can love myself! I assure you this is all that the underdeveloped countries are saying in the end. Provide them then with conditions of love and trust, and together with them you can develop their immense resources for all the time to come, and together with them you can go home and sleep in peace.

* * *

DISCUSSION QUESTIONS

1. Comment on these questions from Adams to Jefferson, written in a letter between friends in their old age: "Have you ever found in history a single example of a nation thoroughly corrupted that was afterwards restored to virtue? And without virtue there can be no political liberty . . . . Will you tell me how to prevent riches from becoming the effects of temperance and industry? Will you tell me how to prevent riches from producing luxury? Will you tell me how to prevent

luxury from producing effiminancy, intoxication, extravagance, vice and folly?''
2. What is ethical behavior—for a *system*?
3. Why are the origins of values different around the world? Do these differences mean that "Truth is not One"?
4. What do the concepts of "moral philosophy" and "jurisprudence" have to do with the explanation of an economic system?
5. Do people always seek pleasure and pain? Do some seek pleasure *in* pain (sadists, masochists, hypochondriacs)? Does a free system require a hedonist–utilitarian view of man?
6. Can individual pleasures be added up to achieve the sum of social pleasure? How?
7. Can individual pleasures be compared over time?, or among persons? Would it be useful to do so?
8. Should our material goals be transferred to other cultures that do not share our underlying value system?
9. How can the two be transferred together? Can they be exported?, or only imported by the other country?
10. How can you demonstrate that the two are linked inextricably?

SELECTED READINGS

Beauchamp, T. L., and N. E. Bowie. *Ethical Theory and Business.* Englewood Cliffs, N.J.: Prentice-Hall, 1979, Chap. 1.

Bennet, Bauer, Brown, & Oxnam. *Christian Values and Economic Life.* New York: Harper Brothers, 1953.

Clark, J. M. *The Ethical Basis of Economic Freedom.* West Redding, Conn.: Calvin K. Kazanjian Economic Foundation, 1955.

Green, R. W. *Protestantism, Capitalism, and Social Sciences.* Lexington, Mass.: D. C. Heath, 1975.

Rokeach, M. *The Nature of Human Values.* Glencoe, Ill.: The Free Press, 1973.

Smart, J. J. C., and Bernard Williams. *Utilitarianism: For and Against.* New York: Cambridge University Press, 1973.

Stamp, J. S. *The Christian Ethos.* Freeport, N.Y.: Books for Libraries Press, 1926.

Tawney, R. H. *Equality.* London: Geo. Allen & Unwin, 1952.

Tawney, R. H. *Religion and the Rise of Capitalism.* New York: Mentor Books, 1947.

Chapter 2

Institutions of Capitalism

How are the values discussed in the previous chapter to be expressed in a business or economic system—specifically, the system known as Capitalism? According to the Classical economists, Capitalism is made up of a set of carefully dovetailed institutions, potentially justified by their achieving collectively the values they each pursue. By institutions, I do not mean hospitals, universities, government agencies, and the like. Institutions in this sense are customs, traditions, ways of doing things; in other words, the organized reflection of values. Values *are* organized into social institutions. Society is structured to represent the underlying values. Capitalism's original objectives, in terms of these values, were the freeing of the individual for creative activity and the achievement of his satisfaction—through material growth of the system.

How can you design a system so that the whole society will grow and all individuals will have a chance to be creative, to pursue their individual objectives? Notice the phrasing of the issue: "How do you *design* a system?" One could ask, "how do you pursue values?", but design of the system is at the heart of the matter. Ethics are *values in action* in systems, not merely in people's minds. How do we *achieve* our values? Something has to be done to put them into operation. We have to make a link, therefore,—an operational link—between individual freedom and growth of the society. Freedom is not just an end; it is also a means to the final goal. It is *used* to achieve other objectives such as godliness (perfection) and the social good. *Individual* freedom is for *social* growth, the growth of the society, as well as for individual evolution. Why must the society grow in order to achieve the values we're after? There has to be growth of the *whole* for the individual to maximize his creativity or pleasure. No single individual can reach his *highest* fulfillment until *all* do. A problem in designing an economic system is how to tie together individual freedom and social (material) growth?

INSTITUTIONS OF CAPITALISM

Capitalism is a system beautifully designed for that purpose, and grounded in explicit ethics. Adam Smith's book, *The Wealth of Nations* (1776), offered an explanation and justification of Capitalism. It was written to explain not the wealth of individuals, but the *nations;* not of the world, but of individual nations. It described a system which makes a national society materially better off. Smith posed the question of how free individuals could be induced to act so that individual effort led to national improvement. His response was an entire system composed of six institutions including—

economic motivation
private productive property
free enterprise
free markets
competition
limited government

MOTIVATION

Smith wrote that man has two motives: greed and benevolence. Benevolence is what the church asks in terms of stewardship. He said men are motivated to give wealth away after they have earned it through capitalistic accumulation. He asked himself if an entire system could be based on benevolence alone, and answered that it was not an adequate motivation for economic behavior. How can a system work in which everybody is giving everything away?

What would the social system look like? Who would work? Who would take time to produce anything? What would they produce?

But, if man's effort, his work, is tied to his reward, he will work. Capitalism is a work-system, based on a work ethic that assumes that work itself is good, and should be done with prudence and diligence. According to *Ecclesiastes*, work is "good," of itself; and *Proverbs* says (and *Job* implies) that if done for the glory of God, it also brings material rewards.

Smith said simply that man works harder if he has an economic return for it. Man is greedy, in other words, and will work harder for more return. But the work *ethic* also says that a man should work regardless of whether he gets proper return. He shouldn't even *seek* a reward. The Old Testament eulogizes a man "who works and doesn't seek rewards"; then he will receive sevenfold. Reward comes to him who doesn't seek, but who does what is his duty. Smith, nevertheless, accepted man's sinfulness and tried to show how it could be turned to the benefit of society.

Smith was a professor of jurisprudence and of moral philosophy. Out of these two subjects came Western economics! But despite his moral preferences—Smith was a Scots-Presbyterian—he realized from observation that the system had to use man's greed as a motor.

Capitalism is based on the assumption that people are motivated by material gain. It *assumes* we can get people to do things by giving them material reward (income). He who works for nothing, or for the pleasure of work alone, or he who works and gives away everything, is an anomaly in the system. Capitalism doesn't know how to handle him. Capitalism is based on the concept of material motivation in which the *more* an individual receives, the *more* he is motivated; the more he works, the more he receives.

Is it true that the greater opportunity a person has to gain, the harder he will work? We know that in some societies, and in some individuals, it is precisely the reverse: lots of people will *stop* working at certain levels of material gain. For example, some members of construction crews quit working for the week when they have enough money. It doesn't matter how much you offer them; they won't come back until they need more money. They're maximizing their pleasure over their pain, because working is pain, and they'll take just enough pain to get the pleasure they're looking for. The motivation assumption breaks down with these people, and when it does, we fuss at them. "You're not motivated right! You don't understand the system! When we pay you *more*, you're supposed to work harder! And you're supposed to work harder to get more!"

A representative of a British company once said to me, "One of our problems is we can't get the women to work harder in the plant. We decided we would have a little motivating session; we called them in and asked them:

'Where do you live?'

'Well, we live in little flats, some of them cold water and so on.

'Wouldn't you like to have a hot water heater?'

'Who does?'

'Wouldn't you like to have a big refrigerator with a freezer?'

'What do we care? We've got a refrigerator. What do you want a freezer for?'

'Wouldn't you like to have a dishwasher?'

'Eh, not too many dishes to wash.'

"We can't make them think of acquiring *things*. They just sit there, working their 40 hours and consuming what they got and letting the State take care of the rest. We can't get them motivated."

Capitalism is based on an assumption that individuals are motivated by material gain for pleasure. This is dangerous ground. We face an ethical issue right here because "material gain" equals "greed" or, avarice. Let's think back a moment! What was avarice to the church in the sixteenth century? A sin, and a *deadly* sin, at that. (Incidentally, what are the other six deadly sins? Anger, covetousness, pride, sloth, lust, and gluttony—all things we like to do.) What is a *deadly* sin, as compared to a sin? In *Paradise Lost*, Milton made the distinction between the deadly sins and the plain old sins in terms of the degree of punishment—the difference between hell and purgatory. With a sin, you could go to purgatory, which on Milton's map is on top of the Earth, on the way to Heaven. You can stay there a while, cleanse yourself, and eventually go on into Heaven. Hell is on the bottom, and with a deadly sin, you just drop right through. There's no stopping in purgatory with one of the seven deadly sins. You go the *other* way.

Capitalism started from avarice—one of the deadly sins—to build a system which was itself ethical. The beauty of Capitalism was that it took a sinful motive and used it to make an ethical system—the neatest trick of the century! Capitalism, as a system to reflect individualism and hedonism, was justified by the social philosophers— Adam Smith, Jeremy Bentham, James Mill, John Stuart Mill, and others—as a "good" system. But the problem with Capitalism is that few people really like it as it was supposed to function.

We have begun to see how Capitalism was supposed to work by motivating an individual who is, by nature, greedy. That tells us something about how to make the system work for social growth. How do you take greed and use it to develop a society that is good? How can you build a system on a concept of man's behavior as sinful, according to our own religious beliefs, and make it work to help *everybody*? The answer is found in five other institutions, which limit and channel the greed.

PRIVATE PRODUCTIVE PROPERTY

We begin with a means by which economic motivation can be exercised. That means is *private productive property*. An individual must have something to be creative with. Private property can be used for private benefit, but the society as a whole should benefit, too. Each individual will greedily use property for his greatest economic benefit: he would not use it as efficiently if someone else owned it and paid him *part* of the fruits of his labor. Private productive property assures that each person reaps the benefit of his own efforts. If everybody works for one man, who alone has all the property, he is the only one with the ability to create. The feudal lord who owned all of the land, the cattle, stables, and so forth—he told the serfs what to do. He could be creative. But the serf who was greedy—what happened to him? He got his hands cuffed! Private productive property is a necessary complement to individual economic motivation. It is necessary for individuals to work effectively, doing the best they can with it, responsibly, and thereby improving the whole society.

Historically, private productive property meant something different than it does today. What are the rights of private property? You can buy, sell, use, but not abuse. You have no right to *abuse* your property, or to use it in certain nuisance ways. What's "abuse" of property? Beating your horse is an example. Strip-mining is another one, depending on the constraints of the law and our value concepts. Another: you can't put up a fence between you and your neighbor so high that it diminishes his right to light and air.

What is the Latin derivation of the word "abuse"? This is a tricky one, but is it important! The prefix *ab* means "out of", "away from." So abuse means you are not permitted *not* to use. Where did that concept come from—that you don't have the right *not* to use your property? This is the *stewardship* concept of the talents. You take the talents given you and *use* them, for the benefit of the master and of society. And you *should* use them, for you are steward over the property of God. Therefore, you have *no* right *not* to use it. We have gotten far away from the original concept of abuse, now defining it as not using property well, as in *"mis*-use." Abuse means also taking away, out of use. Property was "given" for the purpose of supporting the system, or society, and not to use it is not to support the society. A colleague of mine was writing a book on agriculture in the United States and put a picture of the Department of Agriculture in it with the subtitle, "The largest insane asylum in the world." Ninety percent of the Department of Agriculture was helping to increase production and 10 percent was stopping it. A government agency trying to *remove* property *from* use! Absolutely ridiculous! Something has gone wrong with Capitalism when you can make that observation. Something is wrong with the system.

(A small detour: that is why Henry George wanted the single tax—to lay it on the man who wasn't using his property, because to George that was the cause of poverty. There was plenty of productive property out there; it just wasn't used. People were sitting on it for capital gains purposes, and thereby were *abusing* their property.)

We gave up that concept of *non*-use long ago. That act destroyed one of the bases for the justification of private property. The person who can acquire private property and deny the use of it to himself or to anybody else destroys the basis on which the society extended the property right—for property is to be used to benefit the society. This concept is so tied to the property right that the French philosopher Proudhon could argue that "property is theft," because it took God's gifts from the people. There are a good many leftist groups in France that still wave that banner. The property right permits individuals to sit on God's nature. This is a somewhat different idea about the relationship of man to nature: man can withhold the fruits. To prevent this, many countries deny private property rights to the subsoil. Minerals and petroleum are supposed to belong to everybody, so the state owns the subsoil itself.

Private property, therefore, is an expression of individual freedom in the materialistic realm. Jefferson argued that logically *no* society can be *free* which was not an agrarian society; each man had to have "survival land." But Hamilton insisted no society could be *rich* unless it was an industrial society. In their debate during the early years of this nation, Jefferson said, in effect: "You make it industrial, and a man will be a slave to other men; if he lives in an agrarian system, he can spit in the eye of the government." Why? He can always take care of himself. He is accountable to no one but God, who gave him largesse. If the only elements of your economic system were *motivation* and *property*, an agrarian society is about as far as you could go.

Notice, however, that the right of private property is constrained by our religious and philosophical values concerning its use. What is the owner of material goods supposed to do with them? Produce! He's supposed to use them for production; he's *not* supposed to sit on them. And what is he supposed to do with the largesse? Share it, because God gave him the material goods in *stewardship*. Stated philosophically, this means that society gives the individual the right to *use* the property, permitting ownership as long as the property is used for the good of society.

We hear a lot about stewardship in our churches, but we don't really stop to think how deep the concept is in our economic system. The justification for private property *has* to hang on stewardship. Otherwise, what would happen to private property? The right of ownership would probably be taken away, as under socialism and communism. Another reason is that property would increasingly be concentrated in the hands of the more capable or fortunate few. Under Hebrew law, any land that was sold reverted every 50 years back to the owner, in order to keep it in the tribe. Thus, there are deep value systems underlying our concept of *how* man should be related to property.

As I said earlier, if our only factors were economic motivation and private productive property, we would have only an agrarian society plus some craftsmen, as in the 15th to 18th centuries. Let's move on to the institutions which are important for industrialization.

FREE ENTERPRISE

Free enterprise is the institution which permits, among individuals, the combination of the elements of production for the purpose of pursuing a particular economic or commercial objective. It can refer just to the use of *your* own property, as well as your use of your property in conjunction with somebody else's. The "free" part of it was a revolt against both guilds and government controls, which determined who could enter what enterprises. The antagonist was the state, which had controlled economic life under the system we now call mercantilism; "laissez-faire" was advocated to reduce or eliminate state interference. Under free enterprise, entry into and exit from *production* is theoretically open and free. It says nothing about the conditions of the market, only the conditions of production.

Free enterprise permits the formation of partnerships as well as individual proprietorships. Individual proprietorship is no more than ownership of private property. Free enterprise permits the combination of properties so people can do things together that they can't do alone. Free enterprise means a capitalistic combination of factors of production under decisions of free individuals. Free enterprise is the group expression of the use of private property, and it permits greater efficiency in an industrial setting through variation in the levels and kinds of production.

Free enterprise functions to combine factors *outside* of the market. That's important to understand: you contractually bind factors together in order not to have to hire them day-to-day in the market. It introduces a desirable stability to the system by relieving you of the necessity of each day having to go out and borrow capital and hire labor. The institution of free enterprise begins to complicate the concept of stewardship, however, for several individuals are now responsible. We will return to this problem later.

Free enterprise is a necessary part of Capitalism in that it is a *means* of expanding opportunities for creativity for the owners and managers, and of letting *all* with ability and willingness produce—thereby expanding the goods and services available to consumers. It may, or may not, expand opportunities for labor—this will depend on what is done in the enterprise, how labor is used, and whether jobs are available.

The institution is so important that our overall system is often called the "free enterprise" or "private enterprise" system. This is a misleading use of the words, however, since they really refer to this one institution only. The *system* is so complex that it requires an iteration of all the relevant institutions in order to encompass it.

FREE MARKET

The *free market* is the mechanism by which individual decisions about pleasure are signaled to the producers, and potential sellers signal their willingness to supply goods or services. The free market operates to equate supply and demand—supply reflecting the *ability* and *willingness* to offer certain goods or services, and demand reflecting the consumers' ability and willingness to pay. Price is adjusted to include the maximum number of *both* bids and offers. The market, therefore, is *the* decision–making mechanism outside of the firm. It is the *means* by which basic decisions are made about the use of resources, and all factors are supposed to respond to it, however they wish. They do respond, but the equilibrium of supply and demand is not the *end*. Clearing the market is not the goal of capitalism; it is merely the function of the market—*any* market. A *free* or self-regulating market is one operating without duress or governmental interference.

The market is not a place where a supplier presses his goods on the consumer in order to clear his shelves. The consumer is supposed to exercise a *free* choice to maximize his pleasure. He is not supposed to be subverted in the maximization of his pleasure by someone saying, "You have to buy." The price he pays must be a freely established price, the translation of increased demand into increased real production to meet that demand. The market has to be *absolutely free* of duress of *any* form. What is passed from the seller to the buyer must be real and useful information—no more, no less. The consumer must have *all* relevant information, on time, and without pressure.

(Let me pause to relate this issue to the effort by the Federal Trade Commission to define "appropriate" information as truthful, timely, and so forth. Why do they have to define this? Why have we had to turn to the Federal Trade Commission to define what is appropriate passage of information? The answer lies in our being unwilling to recognize the necessary elements of a free market.)

According to Adam Smith, information is fundamental to freedom under Capitalism. "The consumer is King" under Capitalism, he said. To satisfy the consumer requires information! The consumer is the only one who should dictate, and the consumer must be well-informed in order to make pleasure–satisfying choices.

In sum, the system has as its objective social service—the growth of material goods and services for the purpose of meeting the needs and desires of individuals who are seeking material gain and who express their demands in the market. Demand and supply were originally seen, therefore, as expressing the free choices of those owning property and those having income to buy the goods.

COMPETITION

Smith went a step further, saying that a free market is self-regulating. An "invisible hand" moves the buyers and sellers so that their market is in equilibrium and the system grows without great trauma. But this occurs only if supply and demand are established under competitive conditions. *Competition* is the fifth institution. If there were only four—a free market, free combination of factors in enterprise, individual greed, and private property, the system would end up in monopoly. It would end up in a hierarchy of powers, with the top occupied by whoever was most persuasive, most aggressive, most capable of applying duress, and so forth. We call the period in which this type of activity existed in the United States the period of the Robber Barons—men who sought great wealth and power and to do so robbed the rest of society. That period is vividly recorded in our history books as one in which the rules were violated.

I am not sure American historians have fully understood the capitalist system or what should have happened in it, but they are certainly good at indicting it. Students, too, are ready to criticize, because they do not understand the social philosophies underlying the economic system—or, perhaps, because they *do*. Most have been imbued with the concept of pure competition as the key that makes Capitalism work to satisfy all individuals. Smith himself saw the tendency to monopoly when he said—that two businessmen cannot pass the time of day on the street without forming a combination in restraint of trade. They will share information which the consumer will not have and, therefore, warp the flow of information and the nature of competition.

For competition to be free, there must be an absence of duress and full, relevant, and timely information. What will assure that this happens? There must be no single enterprise in the market big enough to control the acts of any other seller or any buyers. There must be "atomistic" competition, with many sellers—no one big enough to set the pattern. No one can set simply the price he wishes; he must reflect as well the acts of others. Price leadership, basing point pricing, and so forth, are in violation of competition; our anti-trust laws are grounded on this concept. In a situation without duress, with free passage of relevant information, and numerous small suppliers and buyers, competition will work to maintain a free market and equate supply and demand that reflects the demands of consumers. Supposedly, it will be to the interest of all to play the game the way it should be played.

LIMITED GOVERNMENT

Just in case it doesn't work out that way, there is one more institution—the *Government*—which is supposed to set rules and provide protection for the society and its members. That's all, said Smith, that it should do: it should set the rules, enforce them, and stand aside. But do the rules have to be enforced? Why can't the players see that the system is good? Because of *greed*. O.K., back to institution number one. Back to square one, but square one without the other five destroys the system. Economic motivation in combination with the other five institutions runs the system, but it can't work on its own.

What are the appropriate roles of government under Capitalism? (Notice that the question is posed so that government serves Capitalism, and politics is made subservient to economics and business. This is a decided reversal of pre-eighteenth-century patterns in Europe.) First, rule setting by the legislature; second, rule enforcement by an executive or judiciary, through enforcement of contract, and so on; and third, protection of life and property, by the military and institutions of law enforcement. The three branches of government are needed to make the system work—not to *interfere* with it— just to make it work under agreed-upon rules. The most extensive role of the government is to protect. What becomes the concern of the players if the government doesn't protect? What's your first concern if the government isn't protecting the society? Self-protection! You would create your *own* protective system, and that begins to destroy the free play of competition. With these three functions, Smith said, government need do nothing else.[a] He did say that the government might provide free education for the populace, if it wished. Why?—so they would be more informed about what they want and what they can do, and thereby become more productive. It would probably be a better society, he said, if education were provided, but he did not consider it one of the essentials. America made education an integral part of our system at the insistence of Jefferson and some others who saw it as the basis of an informed electorate, rather than informed consumers. Notice that this is a constrained government, and a government which has as its basic purpose the support of a system under which *individuals* are responsible.

Business in this country has never gotten over that concept of the role of government. By this I mean it has accepted the definition and wishes that's where government would stay—in those constrained activities, so long as it's not *too* aggressive in enforcing competition. Government, however, has expanded significantly. Why? One reason arises from problems *not* addressed by the institutions of capitalism—

---

a. He did accept the desirability (not the necessity) of at times interfering in foreign trade by imposing barriers to imports—but *only* to nurture "infant industries" offset an "early start" gained by more industrialized countries, or maintain national security.

some problems were assumed away—and in the rejection of responsibility by individuals.

ASSUMPTIONS UNDER CAPITALISM

Several basic assumptions were expressed or implied in the early discussion of Capitalism. One is the existence of full employment, dependent on flexible wages and prices. In a free market, the prices of goods and labor would move so that all labor was employed; unemployment would be rectified in a short period of time. If there is unemployment, wages will fall—and they will fall enough for somebody to find it advantageous to employ workers. Even if prices are falling, wages are eventually going to fall farther. It may take a little while, but it will happen. The more flexible that wages and prices are, the more ready is this adjustment. Since the market was supposed to be free, full employment was *assumed* to exist. It *had* to be assumed to exist, incidentally, for the system to be ethically justified. If anyone is left out of employment and can't meet his pleasure-desires, or even survive, then individualism goes out the window. If full employment does not exist—and by full employment I'm including all structural and technological unemployment, mobility unemployment, and so on[b]—freedom does not exist. It doesn't mean that everybody must be employed 100 percent of the time; it merely means that there are jobs available and unemployment is transitory. If workers don't take the jobs, that's up to them. Voluntary unemployment is not counted. But, for a system of Capitalism *not* to have jobs available for people is itself a condemnation of the system, since its overall objective is for the individual to be creative and to pursue his relationship to God and society with the material things at his disposal. If there is no job, or no property, then there is no choice. And without choices, people are not free.

Freedom is defined as choice. He who has no choices is a slave or a prisoner. Even then one choice remains—to live or die—but that's not a choice we include in assessing freedom. Since the goal of individual freedom requires choices, the 18th and 19th century social philosophers had to assume the existence of full employment.

There is another root to this assumption of full employment. These men were not blind when they looked around and *saw* unemployment. How could they explain this? How could they possibly

b. Concepts of full employment are becoming increasingly complex and fuzzy, with multiple bread-winners in a family, and individuals moving into and out of the work force. But we need not bother with these details here.

justify the existence of unemployment when the system wasn't supposed to permit it? Being *moral* philosophers, some of them decided that the answer was sin on the part of the workers. The thesis went this way: "There is only so much work to be done in any given period of time, and there is only so much money to be paid for wages. If there are too many workers, one of two things will happen: either some will be unemployed or all will earn too little." Too little meant not enough to live on.

Observing the poverty even of those who were employed, they said, "People are employed, but they're poverty stricken. Some of them are dying. There must be a reason." Their answer: workers are sinful. They are slothful, they are indolent, they are lustful and licentious; avarice they may have, but not a will to work. It's those other things that are getting in the way. Therefore, Parson Malthus said, "If you people would stop propagating, you wouldn't have so many children going into the work force and reducing wage rates." In the 18th century, children went into the work force at a very young age, at 10 or 12, even 7 or 8. Malthus said, "If you workers would stop propagating all the time, and spend your time working instead of in bed, working instead of drinking, you'd be more productive, and everybody would be better off." Subsistence wages and poverty, in other words, were the direct result of sin. This sentiment is still expressed today in the argument against welfare and in favor of workfare.

The second assumption was that all factors of production are appropriately treated as commodities—that there is no relationship between man and his work other than the significance of the wage and the definition of the job. Hence, there is no satisfaction (value) to be gained out of work *other* than the income of money wages. Work has no meaning outside of the contractual relationship. This assumption means that *work* is not *life;* on the contrary, work is pain. It separates man from his soul. I call that an assumption; it is not only an assumption—it is a cavalier concept of life. In some African countries there is no word for work. I first learned that from somebody who commented, "See they'll never understand how to progress; they don't even know what work is." What the writer did not understand was *why* there is no word for work in those African societies. Why not? Because work is not separated from life—not contracted out. When somebody does what he is supposed to do— goes hunting, or fishing, or builds a hut, or digs a trench, he doesn't go "to work." There is no such concept. It's not work, but merely one function in life. The concept of work comes from contracting out.

Capitalism assumes that work is separable from life. In a larger sense, *industrialization* assumes that work is separable from life, whether it be capitalistic, socialistic, or any other system of industrialization. Jefferson's concern was valid, for industrialization does separate production from consumption and life from work.

The third assumption was that those receiving income under the system would accept their rewards as "appropriate" or "equitable." The basis of income in this system was that it was received according to contributions of each individual, as valued in the market. Nothing forced the workers or property owners, however, to like the distribution of income. Ricardo built theory of income distribution based on the conflict of land-owners, capitalists, and workers over their share of income. Obviously, this conflict could spill out of the market into the political arena—and it did.

These underlying assumptions of capitalism were critical for they quickly began to break the system. As concerned people looked out at the effects of capitalistic industrialization in Britain, the first laws they passed were to help the poor. They recognized that something was wrong when people are poor and people are starving. The system was not working to provide full employment at a survival wage.

If you go back and read the debates of the 1830s and 1840s in Britain, you will find concept-for-concept what has been said recently in Congress on the welfare program—almost word-for-word. One hundred and thirty-five years later we have learned little of the problem of poverty and income distribution. We are still making the same arguments and coming up literally with the same pallid solutions. These solutions were tried 135 years ago and didn't work, and now we're trying them again. The efforts to help the poor worked so badly, in fact, that the British Poor Laws of the 1840s were not to help the poor but to take away public support and force them into the factories.

(As a sage said, "The only lesson we learn from history is that we never learn from the lessons of history." This is true in the United States partly because we do not really study history: Americans do not really believe in history; we believe only in creating the future, as in "Today is the first day of the rest of your life." Americans don't like to think that "Today is also the last day of the past of your life and the link which anchors the future to the past." It's important, however, to think about the past and the present because it helps us understand the future.)

Back to the concept of labor as a commodity! European and

American labor has said for the past hundred years, "We are not a commodity to be bought and sold in a market." Labor accordingly began to work for its goals outside the market system and thereby changed the rules of the game, including the distribution of income. To maintain full employment, the government has been given the responsibility for regulating the level of economic activity. This and other modifications have been made in the system to correct for problems which were assumed way. As a professor of mine at Davidson College said years ago, "it is precisely those things you do not know that will hurt you; not the other way around." This is what's happened to capitalism. There were some things we didn't know and didn't really want to know. Malthus argued the possibility of unemployment, but Ricardo was more persuasive in arguing the existence of full employment—or the (theoretical) impossibility of unemployment. Capitalism has thus changed radically since its conception, and that is the subject of the next chapter.

DISCUSSION QUESTIONS

1. How is an economic system designed?
   a. Does it have to have goals and *criteria* of perfection and achievement?
   b. If so, how are these determined for a society as a whole?
2. Why are the particular institutions of capitalism so closely tied? How can they be made to work?
3. What are the justifications for private property?
   a. For ownership of sub-soil rights?
   b. Why not of air and space above the ground also?
4. What are the opportunities of the "propertyless"?
   a. How can they be "creative"?
   b. Is full employment required?
5. What must "effective full employment" mean for a system to provide individual freedom?
   a. Who should be counted as employed?
   b. Is our measurement of unemployment appropriate?
6. What are the motivations of managers?
   a. How do they alter the working of the economic system or business itself?
   b. How can motivations be altered?

SELECTED READINGS

Beauchamp, T. L., and N. E. Bowie. *Ethical Theory and Business.* Englewood Cliffs, N.J.: Prentice-Hall, 1979, Chap. 2.

Clark, J. M. *Economic Institutions and Human Welfare.* New York: Alfred A. Knopf, Chaps. 5-9.

Heilbroner, R. L. *The Worldly Philosophers.* New York: Simon & Schuster, 1953.

Hirschman, A. O. *The Passions and the Interests.* Princeton, N.J.: Princeton University Press, 1977.

Stepelevich, L. S. (ed.). *The Capitalistic Reader.* New Rochelle, N.Y.: Arlington House, 1977.

Wagoman, J. P. *The Great Economic Debate: An Ethical Analysis.* Philadelphia: Westminister Press, 1977.

Walton, C. C. *Ethos and the Executive,* Englewood Cliffs, N.J.: Prentice-Hall, 1969, Chaps. 1-3.

Ward, A. Dudley (ed.). *The Goals of Economic Life.* New York: Harper Brothers, 1953.

Chapter 3

Modifications in American Capitalism

We considered in the first sessions the ethical foundations of Capitalism and the nature of the institutions which make up that system. We can now observe that the system in its pure form has never existed—because the players would not follow the rules, and the assumptions underlying it were inaccurate. Full employment was not maintained, and even when employment existed, some people were too poor to survive. This meant that some serious social problems were not resolved under the system, and adjustments had to be made. The means to create full employment and eliminate poverty have not yet been found—not recognized or applied—, and we continue to face these problems without adequate tools. Yet under the ethical precepts of capitalism, a man cannot be free unless he has the wherewithal to maintain himself and his family—not that he is guaranteed a job, but that he has an opportunity to survive, be creative, and perfect himself.

But remember that capitalism was directed at (designed for) material growth on the assumption that such growth would *permit* other creative acts. It was designed as a system for which the central goal was growth of the material welfare of the nation—and hopefully for all nations—with the engine of the system being personal and selfish economic motivation. The system was not designed for the growth of mere happiness but rather happiness which arose from material welfare. This material welfare is measured cardinally by the increasing accumulation of goods which are valued in the market.

The major technique for growth under capitalism—and the origin of its name—is *capital accumulation* and investment. Growth is presumed to occur from the lengthening of the processes of production—through increasingly complex stages and specialization—which requires in turn the accumulation of capital to produce the machinery and equipment to permit specialization. All industrial societies, in fact, are capitalistic in their structure in the sense of using capital accumulation to permite more complex stages of productions. What distinguishes the system called Capitalism from Socialism, Fascism, and Communism is *not* its use of capital, its level of industrialization, or its complex specialization. Rather, it is its distinct institutional structure and its reliance on the individual and his personal motivations to accelerate the growth of the society as a whole.

But what happened in the system at a very early date was that this personal motivation swamped the growth and development of the other institutions, altering their nature even to the point of atrophy or demise. Of the six institutions which we've discussed so far, only the first, or economic motivation, remains in its pristine glory. All the others have been radically altered from their original concepts. As a consequence, government's role has increasingly been one of interference and regulation as a means of curtailing the ill-effects of individual greed. This greed should have been curtailed by the individuals themselves, but they did not follow the rules of the game.

PROTECTION AGAINST COMPETITION AND THE MARKET

Let us turn to the question of how the institutions of capitalism were altered, leaving us still with the problem of how to advance the society through individual effort. The key concept is "protection," for nearly everyone in the system has wanted to protect himself from its affects.

Industry

In the U.S., protection began in the early days of our society—in 1971 to be exact. Hamilton wrote his *Report on Manufactures* that year, the purport of which was that we must *protect* the American industrialist against competition from the British for the purpose of national growth and welfare. The Republican party stood for years on two platforms—protection against the foreigner and domestic improvements. Domestic improvements meant the government's building the infrastructure for the development of industry—transportation, utilities, and so on. What's wrong with foreign competition, if the competitive system is supposed to work? It's cheaper! The consumer would get something cheaper, maybe better, and that's bad! It means letting imports displace actual or potential domestic production, hurting domestic activity and leaving the country at the mercy of the foreigners in the case of a war.

Even Adam Smith said that there are times in which the national security would need to be protected by interferences in the market. But the term national security sometimes covers a multitude of petticoats. (I use the word deliberately because the U.S. lace and embroidery industry went before Congress during the Korean War and demanded protection from foreign imports for national security reasons. I assumed, when reading about it, that they were in favor of frilling up the WACS to raise their morale. Not so: the argument was that the American soldier could not fight effectively without an embroidered patch on his shoulder, cap, or lapels, despite the fact that the enemy seemed to do pretty well without them.) There were five thousand commodities on the Defense Department list of national security items during the Korean War, two of them being mustard and ketchup. C-rations don't go down very well without mustard and ketchup, so those were national security items. Obviously there are times when we need to protect our producers, but the argument can get absurd.

National security wasn't the real reason for demands for protection. Protection in the United States was for the purpose of building up the U.S. industrial base against foreign competition. The industrialists and Congress said, "We don't want to face certain kinds of competition; they are unfair." The industrialists wished to modify free competition to mean "fair" competition—or as it is frequently called, "fair and reasonable" competition—which was generally interpreted to mean that the foreigner should have his competitive advantage removed.[a] They have continued to claim the right of protection against foreign enterprise, saying in effect that the rules

a. This concept of protection was not an American invention. It was already practiced in Europe. In fact, it had never been fully abandoned in the Continent, having held sway under the guild system and mercantilism. It is free trade that has been the exception—reigning for about 20 years between 1860 and 1880—*not* protectionism.

and institutions of capitalism should be coterminus with the national boundary. Industrialists have sought protection in order to stabilize their production and to raise their profits—and to prevent themselves from being driven out of business by "unfair" competition from abroad. The 1913 tariff used the principle of reasonable competition as the basis for setting tariff rates for all imported goods in such a way that their prices would be equal to domestic prices; only such equality was considered "fair." When sellers are not able to obtain adequate protection through tariffs or quotas, some have requested direct support from the government through such things as subsidies or "buy American" regulations.

This is not to say that other countries do not practice the same tactics. They do. It is only to say that no one really liked the swashbuckling aspect of capitalistic free competition and free markets when it hurt him. We've heard this argument recently with reference to steel, television, shoes, mushrooms, stainless steel flatware, and so on. I am *not* saying this is bad, good, or indifferent; it is simply what has happened. Whether it is good or bad depends on *values*. I am saying that the system was destroyed from within, by those who didn't want to play the game the way it was designed.

The competitive nature of the domestic market was also altered. The 1880s and 1890s marked the period of the great trusts, the purpose of which was to *monopolize* trade by reducing free entry and forcing the exit of some companies. This altered the relations of sellers and buyers. Free competition has as its objective the power of each individual *consumer* to *decide*. But each individual *supplier*, facing free competition, has the objective of control—to drive out the competition or beat it. Free competition, unbridled, will destroy free competition. It will end up with somebody "vanquishing" the competition. Rockefeller, for example, gained control of the market by whatever means were available. Later on, he and Carnegie and others decided they should give some of their gains back to society, and they set up various foundations and charities. Stewardship was a part of their beliefs, but only *after* they got the wealth—just as Smith had said. They did do something good with it. Carnegie, in fact, was a very interesting man, concerned with some of the social problems of the day. He simply played the game by existing modes of behavior—not by the rules as designed. He wished to vanquish the competition, to monopolize industry in order to control prices. J. Gould tried to corner the market for gold. He wanted all the gold in the world so he could manipulate the price. Morgan broke him, with the help of the government, because Morgan could see what was going to happen if Gould got it. That's competition? Well, not quite, when the government is on just one side.

We have permitted industry to go to the government to avoid the results of competition in a very profitable activity. As a consequence, who now goes to the government to reduce the pains of competition? Anyone who thinks he *can* get help: maritime, shipbuilding, airlines, railroads, aircraft, textiles, steel, trucking—you name it—anyone who can get the rules changed to their benefit. A basketball team whose players average seven feet in height doesn't mind if the basket is raised a foot. It may even try to change the rules to that effect, to put everybody else at a disadvantage. What happened in business? The concept of economic motivation (greed) took over without regard for the rest of the rules. Behavior did not follow the rules, partly because they were never understood, so the system was never really Capitalism.

Breaking the rules is considered profitable. One of the first rules to be broken has to do with information. A free competitive market requires the exchange of ready and relevant information. It has also got to be truthful, for if you pass information which is not truthful, you're passing misinformation. Therefore, information under Capitalism requires honesty; you cannot separate the two. If the information you pass is not honest and truthful, you are not informing to the best of your ability. And the market is *based* on information. Note that I said "ability," not "willingness." You cannot be condemned for not *knowing* certain things which are not in the public domain or not available to you. Relevant information requires that you inform the other what you *think* is important that he know. Now, if you don't *know* all the relevant facts, you are not necessarily required to complete the picture. In some cases, such as the introduction of new drugs, the company is required by law to find out the effects, toxicity, and safety of the drug and make these results known. If you know that a piece of information is important and the customer asks you about it, for you to say, "That's unimportant" when in fact you and he both believe that it is—*that* is not passing accurate information. You would better say, from the standpoint of passing information, "I don't know. Maybe you or I could find out."

One of our Executive Program members in former years said later, "I feel sick to my stomach when I sell an insurance policy to somebody who I know cannot read or understand the fine print. I have gone back to the chairman of my company and said, 'We are not serving the consumer when we do this. Shouldn't we write it so (1) he can understand it and (2) he can and will read it and will buy what he wants?'; and his reply to me was—'Do you want to make money or not?' . . . That hurt." This man was not being honest in what he was selling, and he knew it. Now that is a clear violation of the rules of Capitalism. Again, I'm not now condemning what we've got; I am merely saying that what we have isn't "Capitalism," and I am trying to focus your attention on why we got here and where we want to go next—because we *can* design our future.

Agriculture

Let's take a look at farmers. What did they decide was needed to protect them against the system, and why? What was wrong with the system, anyway? They could not accept the distribution of benefits as determined in the market, because farm income fluctuated and was insufficient (inequitable), and furthermore they had the *power* to change the system through political action. One objective was price stability. Was that ends or means? the real goal was income stability and equity, with increases based on a parity formula. "Parity" in this case means equal in relation to *other* incomes, as they rise and fall. In other words, parity means farm income is to be protected *from* the system. This isn't a production system; it is a protection system. It says, "we want protection against Acts of God and the exigencies of the market."

What was wrong with the market? Why isn't a competitive market in agriculture acceptable? It is inefficient. What's inefficient about a competitive market in agriculture? Market signals caused them to plant too much or too little. Farmers were at the mercy of the buyers—exactly what the system was designed to do. The system was designed for the buyer to dictate, but now we say, "no, that's not quite right." It is true that market signals are badly lagged in agriculture. There was in fact imperfect information coming into the market as read by each individual producer. Why? Not because the market wasn't telling them certain things. It told only demand at the moment—not the future—and nothing about other farmers' reactions. The farmer didn't know what the other farmers were doing, so there was imperfect production information coming out. Even if he did know what everybody else was doing, wouldn't each farmer be likely to produce all he could? He would produce still more after a price rise. Why shouldn't he? Yet, in so doing, all farmers were harmed later on if supply vastly exceeded demand. The system did not necessarily produce results which were acceptable for the producers. The market did not, because of poor information and lagged responses, equilibrate the supply and demand.

The 1979 tractor convergence on Washington was by farmers who said they could not accept even the present system of high incomes. Now something is wrong with a market which doesn't produce an acceptable distribution of income. Each farmer responded by producing *more*, borrowing money to buy equipment to raise his productivity. With more capitalistic farming, the number of farms decreased. The size of farms increased, leading to the destruction of the agrarian society which Jefferson said was the key to freedom. The farmers were shoved into an industrial system where they were no longer able to command resources. The system *changed*. I'm not condemning it; I'm merely describing it. Maybe classical Capitalism would *not* be good, but that judgement depends on our values. In any event, the farmers sought protection, and where did they go to rectify the ills of the system? The government. They went outside the economic system into the *political* system, to protect against the vagaries of the system.

Labor

Labor began, in the mid-nineteenth century, to try to protect itself against the damages of the free market—particularly since full employment was not maintained, and even when it was, wages were so low that they permitted little more than mere subsistence. Unions have been more concerned with the distribution of income than they have with selling their labor in the free market. They have denied that labor should be treated as a commodity to be bought and sold, arguing that labor is part of a person't life, and life cannot be bought and sold. Since labor cannot be dissociated from life, labor should be given a "living wage"—which is the basis for "minimum wage" legislation—without much regard to the contribution of labor to the value of the final product.

Of course, given the poor mobility of labor and the absence of full employment, the industrialist hardly offered jobs in a free market. Collective bargaining was instituted, therefore, to alter the results of the labor market in terms of wages. Since the objective of collective bargaining is for labor to gain more—and continuously more—it is clear that this group has no great love for free markets or free competition, even if these institutions operated as Smith described them.

Virtually any group that can achieve its economic objectives outside of a market, through economic or political power, will do so. Power has become much more important than contribution in determining income distribution. (We will return to this topic in Chapter eight.) With all of the major economic groups denying the desirability of free competition, free entry, and free markets, it is no wonder that these institutions were altered greatly.

This does not mean there is no free competition in the U.S., or no free markets, or that all industries and sectors of activities are closed to newcomers. It means that the institutions of Capitalism have been significantly modified by individuals acting as though they had license to behave outside the rules that were described 200 years ago and considered necessary at the time for the system to be ethcally acceptable to society.

LICENSE

The rules of Capitalism were necessary to keep freedom in the system. What's the difference between freedom and license? A license permits certain actions; but the word "license," to have license, has a completely different meaning, as compared to having *a* license. License is privilege, and unrestrained license is unrestrained privilege. License in its purest sense is the "007" syndrome, which says "anything goes." Now, *a* license says that you have a restrained privilege, to do something in a certain way; those who are not so licensed are prohibited from participating. *A* license specifies freedom and defines privilege. *A* license to drive says that you can drive, but you must follow certain rules. You are *free* to drive, so long as you obey certain rules—but you are constrained. If you weren't constrained in driving, if you had *license*, who else would be free to drive? If you had the 007-type license, who else would dare get on the road? You could drive at any speed; you could bump anybody, and run anybody over; nobody is safe even crossing the road. License itself has no restrictions and thereby denies freedom of others. License is not freedom, and freedom is not license. Freedom requires that you play by the rules and permit others the same freedom. Maintenance of a free market, therefore, requires the continuation of some other individual parties in the market. That doesn't mean you have to protect the other fellow. If he fails by his inability, that's fine, and within the rules. If you out-muscle him, that is not within the rules; and without rules there's nothing but license—or chaos.

For each individual, if his objective is greed, it is profitable to break the rules. I was driving a Latin American friend to the airport early one morning. At the corner, I stopped at a red light. He asked me why I was stopping, and I pointed to the red light. "There is nobody around" he said; "I'd never do that." He believed that the rules don't apply if there's nobody around. In other words, if you're not caught, there are no rules. That is *not* a free society; it is a society of license. It means, as I was told when I visited in Mexico, "If you hit anybody, keep going! Don't stop. If you're caught, you would be the rich foreigner and they will rack you up good. So keep moving." My resolution to the problem is not to drive in Latin America, because I don't know the rules, and I don't want to play the way I was instructed. There have to be rules, and the basic rule is *honesty*. Honesty is not only the *best* policy, it is the *only* policy in a free system. It is the only way to protect each of the parties in the system.

CORPORATE PROPERTY

We have seen what happened to Competition, Free Enterprise, and the Free Market. What happened to Private Property? What is the present nature of productive property in the United States? What happened to private property represented a critical shift in Capitalism—one not foreseen by Marx, incidentally—and it made a significant difference in the development of our system and its ability to increase material growth. *Private* productive property has shifted to *corporate* productive property, which the British call *public* enterprise, as distinct from *private* enterprise or *state* enterprise. This shift is recognized in the statement by Irvin S. Shapiro, Chairman of DuPont, that "Big corporations have become quasi-public in nature."

The Capitalism condemned by Karl Marx was a system based on private productive property. Individual capitalists got rich off the workers. When the revolution started, one knew whom to shoot. The identification gets diffused with corporate property. How do you line up 25,000 shareholders of a large corporation? Something else happens with corporate property: not only is ownership diffused: it is *separated* from *control*. Private productive property combined ownership and control in one individual, or a few, in the case of a partnership. Remember that private property was considered a key to the system because individuals could *own* the benefits (rewards) of what was controlled, and *control* could be exercised creatively under *stewardship*. Ownership and control have to be together; or, if they're separated, something has to be put into the system to maintain stewardship—that is, responsibility! All efforts to remedy the situation through corporate reforms will also require social responsibility. There are *no* panaceas that remove the necessity for responsible action—so long as we have a free society, based on the ethical values surrounding individualism.

When an individual owner ran a factory, one knew who was responsible. One of the things that bothered Southerners after the War Between the States was absentee ownership. What was absentee ownership? Carpetbaggers! The South faced ownership and control from the North. Before the Civil War, the factory owner lived in town, meeting the people daily. After the war, the Carpetbaggers (leather was scarce, and traveling bags were made of carpeting) came south and bought up the operations. Then they went back north and owned *in absentia*, leaving some other Carpetbaggers to run things in favor of the absentee owners. In the polemical literature of the South from 1860 to 1890, "absentee ownership" is a key theme. "Some guy up north *owns* our property, leaving somebody down here in *control*—and they're separated—and when we complain about something, we can get no satisfaction from the owner." Individual ownership remained, but it was *absent* and not *seen* as responsible; and thereby not acceptable.

Let's apply this to the corporate structure, in which the corporation has the privileges of an individual but not the responsibilities. The Capitalist system has been changed as a result of this separation. How can one say that the corporation does not have the responsibilities of the individual? Very simply; the corporation is not a citizen. It cannot marry, it cannot vote, it cannot be put in jail; further, *no one* is visibly responsible for stewardship. Managers often say they are responsible only to stockholders, who are too diffused to exercise responsibility and, in fact, are *not* in control. There is not even an institutionalized way of determining whether stewardship exists, for much information is not readily available.

Why has there been such talk about the "social responsibility" of the corporation? What's the problem? The public is beginning to recognize that while an individual is bound by his community ties, the corporate structure does not necessarily have within it a means of enforcing social responsibility. A businessman who was facing a tough problem said to me recently, "I have to live with the people in my town!" What does that say? That he's part of the community. He is going to behave differently than if he were responsible to outside interests. One of the things the University of North Carolina is finding out, with the increasing out-of-state ownership of corporate subsidiaries in the state, is that we cannot get contributions the same way we could when the companies were owned by North Carolinians. Why? Because out-of-state owners have other interests as well. The local managers tell us, "Such gifts are decided by our corporate headquarters. Put your request in along with those from Ohio and all the rest." There is little identification, little felt responsibility. Previously, individuals were looked to for stewardship; and, if it was not exercised, one knew who was slacking.

But isn't a businessman acting responsibly by simply employing labor and producing goods? Nobody, no *individual*, has a *responsibility* under capitalism to employ anybody else, although we may decide that a property owner has the responsibility to hire *someone* to work his property if he is not going to work it himself. He is responsible, rather, *when* he employs, to provide conditions of work acceptable to the society—a living wage, good conditions, and so forth. When the *product* is produced, the owner of the product has a stewardship responsibility in its supply, in terms of maintenance of quality and accuracy of information. Privately, he is steward over the use of his own income, along with everybody else. But *mere* employment and production do not fulfill the responsibilities of stewardship over property any more than did Fagan's employment of the boys in *Oliver Twist*.

The claim that a corporation is fulfilling a responsibility by hiring people is itself a warping of the ethical foundations of Capitalism. It is a statement which you will not accept if the government said the same of its own actions. Let's suppose the President says, "The government is assuming the responsibility of being the employer of last resort, because business is not assuming its responsibility." Your reaction, and mine, would probably be, "What a terrible system we've got if we have to employ people as a 'last resort'." I will not argue that employment is *no* contribution. Employment *is* a desirable contribution, and so are most products. But that's not what we're talking about when we focus on responsibility. And if corporations ever assume full employment in the system as their *own* responsibility, we can be sure that quality and efficiency will fall. Employment is not the *responsibility* of a company under Capitalism. The system should function to provide employment, but no *company* has that responsibility. Yet this is exactly the load the government has laid on companies. Government not only wants companies to employ: it wants them to employ certain kinds of people, with quotas for each kind. Companies reply, "Who's running my business?" Rightly so! This seems to me to be the wrong way to explain responsibility to the society. You have in *our* society a responsibility to maintain freedom by opening opportunities to all qualified. Anything else you may do for the disadvantaged is a matter of charity, in my mind.

There is a responsibility of *any* institution to the society in which it operates, because it lives by the will of the society. No institution can survive without social approval. Otherwise, it will be altered or removed. Since the corporation is a creation of the society, it had better act in ways the society approves. *That* is social responsibility! *That* is "responding to the society." When the corporation asserts that its *only* objective is profit, a problem arises. What's the best way to make profit? To sell good products. Shall I fulfill needs and demands?—or break the rules, as long as I can get away with it? Unfortunately, the latter is a signal that is too frequently given in this society—that breaking the rules is better for corporate (or personal) gain than playing by the rules. What do you think all the ruckus over Bert Lance was about? He didn't follow the rules. Lance says, "I've played within the rules." Congress has said, "not quite." And others have raised further doubts.

I'm frequently asked at this point if it isn't a company's role to maximize profits as its social responsibility. We will return to this question later, but we might as well note here that there is no such thing as maximization of profit. There isn't even *an abstract* concept of maximization of profit that makes sense—other than in *pure* micro-theory. It is literally impossible to maximize profits. There's always a dollar more somewhere!

Even if the term "maximization" includes the understanding that there are numerous constraints, we cannot use the term in the abstract. As soon as we admit *constraints*, we can no longer talk merely about maximization unless we talk about a *constrained* maximization. But even recognizing a constrained maximum is not a useful way of looking at profits, because you don't know when you're at a maximum. There's always *more*, and that's what maximization means—the most! One way to get more is to break the rules. Indeed, there are penalties for breaking the rules, but only if you are caught. A recent Gallup Poll showed that the majority of respondents had the perception that companies break the rules for profit. I'm not saying that that's the way it *is*. On the contrary, I'm saying that the best way to achieve profits is by service, in an honest and direct way. As Benjamin Franklin was reported to have said, "if rascals knew the profitability of honesty, they would be honest out of rascality." But we are too timid to try it. It *appears*, therefore, that W. C. Fields was more accurate when he said, "If anything is worth having, it's worth cheating for." And the perception of many, young and old, is that this is the way in which companies behave. Who can help it, when business keeps saying, "We're out for profit and for maximization of profit, and that is our chief responsibility."

There's a beautiful quotation from Peter Drucker—who I think understands more about what's happening in business in this country than almost any other observer—in which he said, "As long as business keeps talking about business as a profit center and profit maximization, instead of cost centers and production centers and productivity centers; as long as it talks about that, it gets what it deserves."

Don't businesses *try* to mazimize profits? Not really; there are too many complex tradeoffs against profits. For example, I don't think your taking time to read this book demonstrates profit-maximizing behavior, because I don't think you can clearly show that it will maximize profits for your company. On the contrary, it may very well make you a more curious person who will doubt some of the things that your company asks you to do. And that is appropriate, for we are now talking about the future of this country, not just about the future of your company or yourself. We're talking about what is going to permit this country to continue to meet the problems it faces, problems which are getting exceedingly complex and which are not going to be handled by people who say the only thing they have to do in life is to make money or maximize profits— especially when, in fact, they are not so single-minded.

I've discussed this matter of profits and profit maximization with the MBAs I teach time and again. They are fully imbued with the goal of "the bottom line." Their first week of class, I give them an hour or two of orientation in which I say, "If you want to make money, get out of the program right now! Because there's nothing in the MBA Program which is going to teach you how to make money. Making money is an *art*. It is not a science and cannot be taught. We teach management." As the chairman of a large corporation once told me, "I've got an eighth grade education and a feel for money, and I can make more money than any bunch of MBA's you want to send up here with their computer print-outs. I'll just turn those computer runs upside down and around and throw them out, and *make money*." Money is not made out of intellect; making money is the art of knowing how to smell a buck and go after it. That can't be taught, so I doubt that you are maximizing profits in the process of discussing these issues.

We teach managers how to manage in a complex society. Management is the tradeoff of constraints and the seeking of opportunities under an administrative structure. Unfortunately, we teach much more about tradeoffs than we do about opportunities. But management is complex also because no manager or company is in the business only of making money. Making money is ancillary to a large number of activities which make up your life, including the role you play in society, the role you play with other people in management, the perception of the community of what you do, and so on—all of which you trade off frequently against making money, including contributions to United Way. If you say that every contribution you give to United Way is *only* because you anticipate making money out of that contribution, you have said something which many people think of businessmen, but which I certainly do not believe.

There are hierarchies of personal and corporate needs and motivations, and they are very complex. Some people go to the office to get out of the home; some work late so that they don't have to argue with the family when they get home. That has nothing to do with making money; it has to do with happiness. These comments come from psychological studies about what motivates a person to keep working. The evidence is that it often has little to do with making money. Nobody's going to pay him any more. He's working, and it's an excuse for *not* doing certain other things. If *you* work harder, do you expect to get more pay? Maybe or maybe not, depending on the system you're working in. If you think I wrote this book or teach to make money, you're crazy. I can make much more money working with a company as a consultant, I *want* to engage in dialogue on these issues. You do some nonprofitable things with much of your time. Did you ever coach Little League? What did you do that *for*? That isn't making any money. You could have stayed at the office and made another contract, maybe! But your life is too complex. And for businessmen to continue to talk as though profit is the only thing that motivates them is to demean themselves in the eyes of a society which doesn't want it to be that way and shouldn't be encouraged to believe it, because it isn't true.

Why don't we admit that our lives are complex and that we have complex motivations in business? The answer lies in a desire to have a precise, numerical (cardinal) measure of performance. Companies see profit as the only thing they've got to measure by.

In a dialogue with some international managers recently, I heard them assert, "That's the problem with my company. They've got me measured by profit, and I have nothing to do with profit. Profits are set by the guy who is setting the inter-company transfer prices from one company to another and who sets my sales prices; all I can do is screen the operation in between, hoping to make a contribution in cost reduction. Now, that's what I ought to be measured by." (Shades of Drucker's comment!) Yet the company will continue to talk about *profit* as the motivation for each manager. There's nothing wrong with profits, but they are *not* the objectives (the end). They are the lubricant (a means) and a very necessary one, at that. They are the score, but not the game!

Look what happens to the system when profit is *all* that motivates. The market is no longer free, and competition becomes monopolistic. What have you got left? You've got a system motivated by economic gain and constrained by the government—only two of the required institutions of Capitalism—with a lot of non-market *power* exercised in between. That's exactly what we've got today, and it is not acceptable in today's society because of its effects on people and the environment.

Making money is, in fact, ancillary to being in business. If you are in business *only* to make money, you had better get out of where you are. Why? You *probably* could make more money elsewhere because it is *statistically improbable* that you have found the place for maximum income for yourselves. The same is true for companies. DuPont, for years, refused to go into the pharmaceutical business, though it appeared to everyone that it was a potentially attractive use of company resources since that sector was highly profitable. DuPont's reply was, "We are in the chemical business." That's a little different from "making money." If I could prove to you that your company could make more money by liquidating its assets and investing in IBM or ITT, it still would not do it. You are really in the business of doing something which you consider to be an enjoyable, useful, and acceptable way to spend your time, a way that involves the process of production, selling, and the earning of *sufficient* profits to continue. That's rather different from maximizing profit.

If business continues to say that it is trying to maximize profits, it puts itself in the position of the physician who, in the process of examining a patient, answered the phone and said to his wife, "Go ahead and buy the fur coat, honey. We'll get the money somehow." That image has changed our view of physicians. Business does itself harm by emphasizing only one side of a multifaceted activity. To reduce this profit-mazimization concept to its absurdity, ask any businessman—"Why did you play with your child last night? Why didn't you spend time reading the latest business journal? And why did you take your wife out to dinner the other Friday night, rather than work at the office?" We all make tradeoffs against maximizing our income. We do sleep—that's another tradeoff against making money—and how much sleep maximizes profits? We tacitly recognize that money is not the reason for our job, that work is part of life, and that life's values affect the way we make money. It does not please us to be reminded that the Chicago gangster, Al Capone, said "This American system of ours, call it Americanism, call it capitalism, call it what you like, gives each and every one of us a great opportunity if we only seize it with both hands and make the most of it. My rackets are run on strictly American lines, and they are going to stay that way."

Any individual or group who puts making money above life's values is the subject of ridicule, as illustrated by the story of the man on his deathbed, whose wife came in to hold his hand. He said to his wife, "Please, honey, ask my lawyer and my doctor to come now." She replied, "The doctor's just been here, and you've taken care of all legal affairs, and you know you have only a few hours." He insisted, so she called them and they both came. As they walked in, he said, "Please, sit one on each side of me." They did so for a while and, finally, his wife couldn't take it any longer. She leaned across and whispered: "Honey, why? Why your doctor and lawyer?" And he said, "Well, after all, the good Lord died between two thieves!"

To me, that gives the *coup de grace* to the argument that it is acceptable *solely* to pursue money or profits. People see the legal and the medical professions as identified increasingly with the pursuit of money—to the jeopardy of patients and clients. As that occurs, their standing in the society, and the professional attributes which we grant them, are being reduced. Professions are becoming downgraded, and now the FTC is permitting them to advertise, and act like any *other* supplier in a market.

What's the nature of a profession? First, it declares itself to be dedicated to *service*. If you run through all of the attributes of a profession, there will never be a mention of money. Why? Money income is supposed to result from service and not be sought for itself. A *professional* life includes complex contributions to society—as does a managerial position. Why is it that we continue to act as though the money indicator is the measure of success for managers—and not for doctors, lawyers or teachers? Why is it? Because we have accepted in full the *assumed* motivation of materialism and have forgotten the constraints which are placed on it. This is why Wendell Wilkie (Republican presidential candidate in 1940) despaired of a society in which "some guy can go dig a hole in the ground and pump black liquid out, become a millionaire, and automatically be considered an expert on everything from politics to petticoats."

The concept that money determines the worth of the individual and is the appropriate measure of success is deep in our society. It is, incidentally, reflected in the statements of our founding fathers. Who was supposed to have the vote in our society? Rich, property owners, who were wise because they were rich; and any wise man was automatically good. "The rich, the wise, and the good" were to have the vote. How did you find out who was whom? Measure his income or wealth. It says so in the Old Testament: Who is wise? He who follows God. And what will God do for him who follows Him? Reward him. Job got his wealth back tenfold because he followed God. The story says that if you are good and show wisdom in following God, you will be rich. All one has to do to find the godly is reverse the sequence and look for the rich! In our society, we expect leaders to be good men and women, but the idea that the rich are good or godly has faded. And one of the results has been the progressive loss of decision-making to the government, which we have relied on to *constrain* unbridled profit-seeking.

ROLE OF GOVERNMENT

Under eighteenth and even nineteenth century capitalism, the role of the government was expected to be fairly small—"that government is best which governs least"—and essentially one of supporting the interests of business. It was to set the rules and to protect business as well as the lives of individuals and the security of the nation. The responsibilities of government were delineated by Smith as provision of personal security (police and fire), national security, and a judiciary for protection of property, competition and contract; a legislature, of course, had to pass the rules and appropriate funds for each.

For the past hundred years, however, government has increasingly interfered in the system for the purpose of redressing the inequities which have developed as a consequence of the game not being played by the original rules. It has interfered also in order to compensate the fact that the assumptions underlying it were not accurate in the first place.

In 1945, the U.S. government began to take responsibility for maintaining full employment; it has not really done so to date. Nor has it found a way of removing the inequities of poverty in the system, and it is not likely to do so for some decades.

Thus, a large amount of the growth of governmental influence in the system has resulted from the need to offset or to constrain the activities of business which violated the tenets of pure Capitalism. Another set of interferences arose from the governmental responses to the requests of various economic groups for protection. The government has thus upset the capitalistic system and tried to right it at the same time. For example, the Department of Agriculture has been trying to accelerate growth through the spread of better techniques of farming, while at the same time it has subsidized farmers who took land out of cultivation and put it into so-called land banks. This last would undoubtedly be an *abuse* of private property under a pure capitalist system.

The government has dealt itself further into the game through its own purchases, accelerating growth of the larger corporations. At the same time, through the Justice Department, it has sought to reduce the concentration of companies or to break some of the larger units into smaller pieces. All this under the assumption that "competition is *per se* good"—that is, competition is an end in itself and should not be traded off against any other "value."

The government has also entered into a large number of areas where business finds itself inadequate to supply *social* needs, though it may supply market demands. Government provides not only the basic infrastructure such as education and transportation. It has also supported communication, air transport, sea transport, housing, welfare, medical services, urban development—and imposed a host of regulations in all fields of business. A long list of regulatory agencies confronts business with a myriad of reporting responsibilities ranging from minority hiring, to safety, to security transactions, and transfers of technology to foreign countries. At one point, in 1977, Secretary of Commerce Juanita Kreps stated that she would institute a bureau within the Department to receive reports on the social responsibility of business—to keep track, that is, of what companies do to fulfill their responsibilities, with the implication that government might help determine what responsibility companies have to the society. She backed off of the proposal rather promptly. Even so, the role of government in the economy and society since World War II can be depicted by an exponential curve of growth of agencies and activities—though the percentage of GNP channelled through the government has been rather stable over the past few decades.

What we have today in "modern capitalism" is neither the capitalism of the Classical type—as justified by Adam Smith and sought these days by conservative economists such as Milton Friedman—nor has it yet been pushed into socialism. It has remained in altered form because it has been quite successful in achieving the major goal—material growth! In fact, capitalism as practiced in the United States has been among the *most* successful of systems in achieving that particular goal. One of our present problems with the system is the addition of other goals. "Man does not live by bread alone," as the saying goes, though it certainly helps for starters. We probably could not afford some of the other goals in the absence of the material success of our form of capitalism.

Our present system has been indicted on several counts for not supplying the "other" goals of life, which include, at the very least: equality of opportunity for each individual to improve himself materially and otherwise; protection of the environment for future generations; the reduction of poverty and production of goods needed for mass consumption; equitable income distribution; nondiscrimination; and others.

Some of these maladies arise from individuals or groups being unwilling to play by the rules. Others, simply because they were not addressed adequately under Capitalism. For whatever cause, the existence of unresolved problems will mean a continued effort on the part of various groups to rectify the situation. This implies an increasing role of government, to which we will turn in the fifth chapter, following an examination of the shifting emphasis on certain values and goals in the society.

DISCUSSION QUESTIONS

1. Was capitalism a well-designed system? Or was it an apology for *laissez-faire*, to get rid of government interference and never really intended to work?
2. Where does private productive property still exist in the U.S. and how significant is it?
3. How should the corporation be structured to be socially responsible (or responsive)? If it cannot become so, what is likely to happen to it?
4. Are personal freedoms tied to freedom of enterprise?—or are they divisible?
5. With a business system based only on greed and governmental control—both exercised through the corporation—what does the future look like?
6. Can man be motivated by other than greed?—
   (a) Is he capable of evolving past this single stimulus?
   (b) If so, what will be substituted and how long will it take?
   (c) What is the process of evolution?
   (d) Does socialism have the answer?

SELECTED READINGS

Bell, Daniel, and Irving Kristol. *Capitalism Today.* New York: Mentor Books, 1970.

Berle, A. A. *The 20th Century Capitalism Revolution.* New York: Harcourt, Brace & World, 1954.

Chamberlain, John. *The Roots of Capitalism.* Indianapolis: Liberty Press, 1976.

Donaldson, Thomas, and Patricia H. Werhane. *Ethical Issues in Business.* Englewood Cliffs, N.J.: Prentice-Hall, 1979, Pt. II.

Harrington, Michael. *The Twilight of Capitalism.* New York: Simon & Schuster, 1976, Chap. 10.

Mason, Edward. *The Corporation in Modern Society.* Cambridge, Mass., Harvard University Press, 1961.

Petit, T. A. *The Moral Crisis in Management.* New York: McGraw-Hill, 1967.

Polanyi, Karl. *The Great Transformation.* Boston: Beacon Press, 1944.

Veblen, Thorstein. *The Theory of Business Enterprise.* New York: Scribner's, 1958, Chap. X.

Chapter 4

Shifting Values of Society

In trying to determine what the *new* design of the system should be, we need to identify the values by which society is likely to judge business activities. Unfortunately for the achievement of a desirable certainty, the values, or weights of values, shift from time to time. And as the social values shift, institutions will have to change. What would *you* say are the social values today? Just run them off. What are the values which we say are good to pursue in our society? Status. Equity. Stewardship. Charity. Justice. What do we *say* we should live by? Honesty, of course. What else? Efficiency. Love. Reverence. Diligence. Progress. Loyalty. Brotherhood. Mercy. Cleanliness. Orderliness. Prudence. Truth. And many more.

VALUE TRADEOFFS

No *one* value is primary over all others. As you can see, some of these values bounce against each other. They conflict. If *justice* is a value? is *mercy* also a value? Yes, but can you have mercy with justice? Some legal scholars will say, "no." Mercy itself means that strict justice is not done: mercy tempers justice. Otherwise, you don't need it. If justice is done, and that is acceptable, then you don't need mercy. But since mercy tempers justice, they are contradictory. Our values are not unidirectional, and as a consequence we have many such conflicts. Can loyalty get in the way of honesty? Certainly. What about the guy who lies to protect the institution to which he is loyal? Attorney General Kleindienst, who lied before Congress concerning a conversation with President Nixon, was charged by the judge with merely being "a little too *loyal* to the President."

If you check through the several values listed above, you'll find something else interesting about them—that we know very little about their specific content. We're never sure what *fairness* is. Love has many manifestations. Loyalty, also. It is virtually impossible to do with the social values what we have done with goals in this society— that is, to quantify them; many are not even describable precisely but can only be illustrated by example.

What's the difference between a value and a goal? Aren't values something you *exercise* in achieving the goal? You don't just sit there with it in your pocket. You *use* it as you go along toward your goal. Ethics are "values in action." Loyalty, for example, is something you can carry with you and apply as you pursue your goal.

QUANTIFICATION

The application of values to pursuit of goals is extremely difficult, however, because of one aspect of the goals. The *goals* in our business society tend to be ones we can *quantify*. Even in governmental programs, goals are quantified: how *many* people did the doctor cure?; how many cavities did the dentist fill?; how many of a minority group have been hired? Never mind merit or capability or social cost; we seem impelled to *quantify* targets. But the social values are not quantifiable. Professionals and businessmen are now being asked to *reconcile* non-quantifiable values with quantified goals. That's where social responsibility comes in, because the unconstrained pursuit of the quantified goals will destroy the system of individual freedom!

How many people do you put on a dialysis machine? Everybody who *needs* it, or only those who can afford it? Should you maximize the number of dialysis machines? Ability to pay is one criterion, but it isn't always used by hospitals. Tradeoffs are made instead. And what are the criteria by which people are making those tradeoffs? *Should* people be kept alive in hospitals through agonizing life— what's the definition of "life" or "living", anyway?—regardless of their inability to contribute to society or to their own well-being? Somebody's got to make these decisions. What are the criteria by which they're made? The social values have to be relied on—and they are not quantifiable. (We return to this problem in Chapter 10.)

We must begin to think of our roles in our decision-making—in business, in our human lives—as integrated more complexly with the *total* society than we have done in the past. That's one of the changes we have to face. We are being asked to consider increasingly complex tradeoffs in our decisions, such as environmental protection and concern for future generations.

Coming back to the matter of maximization of profits, obviously maximizing for *today* might very well be *mini*mizing for the future. The substitution of long-run profits for short-run profits does not help in defining the concept of "maximization", or even of "optimization." Values of continuity—generation to generation—have to be included. They are being forced on us, and a tradeoff is required. For some, *minimum* profit for today is required to be able to *reach* the future—for continuity, at least, and to permit profit for growth and expansion in the future to meet needs of the society. Now we're talking about a completely different concept than *simple* profit maximization. When the oil companies were criticized for windfall profits from the 1973 embargo, what did they say they would do with the profits to try to justify them? They said: "We're not going to keep these profits. We'll put them into exploration." In other words, "See, we have a justified use for them." This observation introduced the complexities of *acceptable* profits, and I would argue that business has not done a good job speaking about them. Nor has it had a very good audience.

Most of the audience has been taught the concept of profit maximization in microeconomics courses, which don't make the distinctions between different kinds of profits or the constraints that are on them. (I used to teach those courses myself, so I know what is in them.) Profit cannot be the *goal*; profit is the *score*! Colleges don't play football for the score; they play football because it involves healthy competition, and the score tells you the results of the plays in a game. The score is not the objective of the game. If that were the objective, we could achieve it more simply by spinning a little dial and saying, "We got 30 and you got 6!" The objective of the game may be winning, but it is winning in a particular activity played by accepted rules—otherwise it's a false or fraudulent win.

MAN'S POSITION

Let me illustrate the shift in concept that I'm talking about. I was in a church not long ago that was filled with banners. One of them said, "The Glory of God is Man." It implied that there is no greater glory. The firmament is unimportant; the earth is unimportant; the universe is unimportant; but *the* glory of God is man! Where does that put man? Next to God. He's not even lower than the angels, anymore, which is where the Bible placed him. It doesn't even include the angels.

Conversely, in a television program on Native Americans, a Navaho said, "We think the White Man has some things to learn from us." He then went on to make this statement: "Man is a Link between the Spirit and Nature." That's a completely different concept of man's place in the world. I am willing to argue that what is happening to the social values in our society is that the Indian concept will become more widely accepted than the Protestant—that man does *not* command nature, and will recognize increasingly that he is *subject* to nature. You might insist that man always has been subject to God and nature. In the view of all religions, he always *is* subject to God, or to the Spirit. I'm talking about his *recognition* of it. I don't care what your concept of God is. That doesn't interest me at the moment, at least, whether you call it "the Spirit" or "the basic laws of nature" or "the All Powerful," "the Ultimate Reality," "The Force," the "Ever-Ever," or whatever. It makes little difference in *this* discussion, because this is about man's being an integral part of a totality, rather than its detached controller.

What we are finding increasingly these days is that man has to accept constraints upon himself, whether they be from nature, or man himself, or God-given. I, personally, do not distinguish between them. We have much to learn from Native Americans, as well as from some other philosophers.

I may sound as though I think we can do without money pursuits. "'Man does not live by bread alone,'" you remind me, "but it sure helps!" Or as another saying goes, "The only thing you can't buy with money is poverty." That's true, but what our society has been saying is that bread will get you *everything.* I'm not condemning the past, or the achievement of great advances by the pursuit of monetary gain. Our society may have had to go through a period of unconstrained pursuit of money in order to break through the wall of material scarcity and to open new vistas. It is perfectly conceivable that man had to be *educated* through the period we call Capitalism, and that we *had* to have this time of extreme individualism and creativity, in order to understand the problems that are created by it. Even Karl Marx had some complimentary things to say about the engine of growth in Capitalism. He pleaded, in fact, for *more* exploitation of labor, in order to provide jobs, increase capital accumulation—and hasten socialism. But we cannot evolve in the future by the methods of the past. Things are going to *have* to change, and they will. I don't know which way they're going to change yet, but I do know that even our concepts of some of the values dear to us— progress and efficiency, for example—will change.

EFFICIENCY AS A VALUE

Efficiency is included in our list of values; it is usually one of the first suggested by managers. But is efficiency *good*? I challenge you to *prove* that efficiency is good.

What is your definition of efficiency? "The least-cost input for the maximum value of output." Is that acceptable? Does it *prove* that efficiency is good? (There are societies which do not believe that efficiency is good.) I am raising the concept to an absolute to remind you, from the earlier discussion of values, that we have values we believe in but which are unprovable as absolutes. They are what we call "situational," "relative," or "culture bound." Under certain situations, in certain societies, and for certain objectives—efficiency is good.

Is maximum efficiency *always* better than some lower degree of efficiency? One uncertainty in the concept is what is included in the inputs and outputs. If I include only one input in my calculation, and measure all of the efficiency with reference to that one thing, I really haven't measured efficiency, have I? There are many more things that *should* go in. Nor do we, in our economic system, put all of the cost factors into the input/output calculation when we consider the value of GNP. If we don't, how can we talk about cost efficiency? There are a lot of things that should go into GNP that we decline to measure. And yet we talk about efficiency as though it is good. I'm not trying to indict our actions. I am taking some fairly strong positions to get you to think about what is happening to business and to our society.

At present, I'm trying to demonstrate that things we raise to the level of "good" are often beliefs. They are not proven. We get them from concepts of pragmatism. We say, for example, "Our company makes more profit in this way," by thinking in "these terms," and it "works!" Americans say to the rest of the world—to Asia and Latin America—"You want to be rich? Then copy our system, because it works!" They say, "It isn't 'good'." And we say, "What are you talking about? It works, doesn't it?" It may be better than anything anyone else has in *our* view, but there are many in the world who don't believe it is *better* than obtaining what *they* want in *other* ways.

Although they would like to have some of the things we have, they don't want to obtain them by the system we have. They would like to have *some* of our results—with *their* values. It is easier for most of the world to agree that two plus two equals four, than to agree that efficiency is good. There are even areas of the world where uncertainty is so imbedded in the values that the people will reply that "two and two are seven, minus three and a half, plus a little something." I am merely asking you to recognize that the idea that efficiency as a value *in itself* is a belief built into our system because of the way in which we *want* the system to work.

Efficiency, as a concept, is related to results; as a value, therefore, it is *relative*. If I try to do something "efficiently," and I don't get the result I want, I *didn't* do it efficiently. I've got to get the results. Some economic systems penalize inefficiency; others don't. You can produce a Rolls Royce inefficiently, or you can produce it efficiently, and still get the same Rolls Royce. A few years ago, Rolls Royce airplane motors were being produced for a U.S. company— good motors, apparently—but they were doing it inefficiently. So the market system penalized them for it. Other systems won't penalize you for that. In fact, one of the problems with the British Rolls Royce engine was that the system of state controls didn't penalize their inefficiency. They were penalized only when they tried to sell the product across national boundaries.

One of our explanations for what is "wrong" with the British system is that they do not consider efficiency a fundamental value— only a "good thing," to be achieved without harm to other values. Sometimes, efficiency is bad, in other words. At least, many Britons do not consider their system undesirable. Efficiency is seen differently by different groups, and its characterization changes over time. It is a shifting, relative value.

The concept of efficiency is complicated by conflict with other value-goals. Production efficiency is made difficult by the effort to pursue certain concepts of equity in personnel policy. I am quite sure that many of you have kept individuals in your plants or companies when you know they are no longer efficient. You are saying, somehow, that efficiency is not good—or at least not *always* good, not absolutely; there are tradeoffs. These tradeoffs make the application of values difficult.

For example, the most efficient way to produce humans in the next decade may be in the absence of the male—through artificial insemination of some sort—or even without a sperm. But we may *prefer* to continue with copulation. Some will also say that it isn't right, ethically, to eliminate the male, for it will lead to tinkering with genetics. We have already raised the problem of genetic experimentation and engineering to moral, or ethical, levels.

Let's confuse the issue further. You're not supposed to eat your fellow man, right? But even the Catholic Church has not condemned those who have done so in some dire circumstances. That runs against deep grain! Ethically, cannibalism is something you just don't do. Yet athletes did it in the Andes of Chile—of course, they ate the flesh only of those who were already dead—and the world was not shocked. Indeed, the men were later blessed by the Pope for doing what was necessary.

I am trying to shake you up a little on the applications of values. Western man believes that we can achieve what is right by intellectual and technical effort. This is a belief in rationality and science—in positivism and pragmatism—and it is a belief that is restricted to the West. It is a Western idea that rationality is the way to meet all problems efficiently. We will, at times, do things *in*efficiently in order to pursue other values such as loyalty, charity, and so forth. All values are tradable against others—at least at the margin. This leads to the necessity of judgments, of using wisdom. We will certainly need wisdom in facing the application of shifting values in our society, and in determining which values are appropriate.

CUSTOMARY VALUES

Before we leave the subject of shifting values, I want to raise the question of justification for illegal or unethical behavior based on the fact that others do it and get away with it, and thereby set a precedent. A popular defense against charges of corruption in business or government these days is "not guilty by reason of conformity to custom." In this type of defense, you don't deny you did it. You just point out that you are upholding precedent. Witness Governor Mandel's defense of his conduct in office by citing the political skull-duggery of former Governor and Vice President Agnew. Mandel said that the practices for which he was investigated were already well established before he was elected to public office in Maryland! To my way of thinking, "conformity to custom" is a naked plea and should be recognized as such by the courts. Yet we frequently seem to think that what *we* do is acceptable simply because "others" do it. How *many* others, and who? Does it make any difference *how* many acted in the same way? (How many times have you told your children, "It doesn't *matter* what the other kids are doing, I expect you to behave. . . . "?)

Many managers feel that if they don't conform to custom they will lose business. As one manager told me, "My boss and I take an annual trip to New York to visit a major customer. We have dinner and a fat envelope is presented to the buyer with $100 bills. We say Happy Birthday—which it isn't—and everybody smiles, but I got sick to my stomach! If we didn't do it, we wouldn't get the business, because plenty of others would be glad to kick in!"

The justification for an illicit act based on widespread practice raises some acute problems. It implies that the rules of the game are being changed and that the ethics of the past should be accepted in the present and future. A consideration it's important not to overlook in this context is that judgment relies solely on experience, which is what most people rely on to guide them in the future, and past experience may mislead you. Things are changing at such a fast pace that values cannot adjust commensurately. This is one of the problems of implementation of values, or even knowing what they are, for business's relationship to society *is* changing, and interpretations of the changes will differ. And not everyone exercises judgment with clean hands. Thus, the agony of a Congress judging the acts of Watergate. Similar conflicts arise in journalism (search for profit or truth?), and attacks on business come from (ethically pure?) academic circles. Business sees itself attacked by sanctimonious people that really don't act any differently—who espouse one set of values and act otherwise. Consequently, business becomes defensive in being singled out as *the* bad guy in society.

I have not yet been invited to give a series of talks on ethics to the faculty of my university, but a number of us at the University of North Carolina and Duke University have been sufficiently concerned to engage in several seminar discussions on applications of ethics to teaching and university life. The Dean and I have talked about our school's ethics—about what we are *not* doing to incorporate a sense of responsibility among young professors, for example. There are professors who think they can cut classes, regardless of the situation, because it's their right to go off on consulting trips to earn additional income. Professors are also responsible for grade inflation and slipping standards of excellence. Academics have just as much problem with ethical behavior as business, but it happens that a discussion of university ethics or the morality of doctors and preachers wouldn't hit home to managers as directly as a discussion of business ethics.

In focusing on business, I recognize that it may appear like the Democrats sanctimoniously attacking the Republicans, and Republicans snickering under their breath about the things Democrats did in the campaign. Instead, each side needs to examine carefully what should be done. That is why these discussions are directed at the issues in, I hope, a non-adversarial way.

I will be taking some very fairly strong positions, at times, in order to focus on the issues. But you will also see that there is a lot of thinking still to be done on each issue. I haven't yet done all the thinking I should, nor will I, by any means. Still there are some areas on which we can focus to help ourselves become *more* capable of answering the kind of problems that are being pressed on business.

DIFFICULTIES OF IMPLEMENTATION

I recognize that even if we understand and accept a given set of values, it is often difficult to implement them. We get caught in what is known as "situational ethics." It is not a happy situation for those who believe in absolute values, for the problem is often more than one of knowing what is *right* in a given situation. The right may be known, but not how to *do* what is right.

The problems of implementation are threefold. First is the limitation of knowledge. What is the situation and *how* should I change it? That is not always clear. Despite assertions to the contrary, few complex situations arise which permit facile answers, ethically. I'm reminded of the cartoon in which several managers are gathered around a desk; one has hit the intercom button and is saying: "Miss Jones, would you send someone in who knows right from wrong?" You may have a set of rules, but you will not know which ones necessarily to apply in each situation. There *are* some just plain absolutes—not lying, for example. Right? That is clear—you don't lie! But there is a difference between lying and not telling something to somebody who shouldn't know it anyway. And there is a difference between lying and simply not telling the truth, the whole truth and nothing but the truth. There is a difference between lying and "bearing false witness" against someone, under oath. (These complexities we will take up in Chapter 7, when we discuss the right to lie.)

The second problem is the inability to produce desired results. One of the very difficult things is to *do* good, notwithstanding your good intentions. You intend to do good by an act, and six other things happen, and the thing is a mess. Then people say, "how can you possibly have . . .?" You cannot always predict the outcome. Aristotle said: "To give money away is easy; to give it away wisely is difficult." Not all persons' expectations of given acts are the same either and people have different skills in making things happen. To *do* good is different from *trying* to do good or from *expecting* or hoping to do good. Remember Don Quixote!

Third is the problem of time, or inability to experiment. You only have *one* chance in most situations. You do it, and that's it! The situation is not there again. You may try to adjust in the future, but that may come out unsatisfactorily—like a referee in basketball making a bad call and then trying to offset it by another incorrect one. The value situations we are talking about are simply not experimental; you can't go back and try it again. You may not face exactly the same situation twice. These problems make it still more difficult to doing things the way society wishes, given the difficulty of keeping up with shifts in social values themselves.

I trust you can see that I do not consider these problems simple, or that one group—managers—is the only one at fault. There is enough blame to go around, for we are all involved in the system and have our votes, in the market and at the ballot box. The question before us now, though, is whether managers will respond to the challenges to their leadership—and how?

DISCUSSION QUESTIONS

1. List the *social* virtues you deem important.
   a. How do they differ from your *personal* virtues?
   b. How can they be reconciled?
   c. Are there priorities among them?
   d. Is either set communicated within your company?
   e. Should they be? Why or why not? If so, how?
2. Does the concept of "efficiency" also include the *value* of whatever is done efficiently? For example, is it "efficient" if resources are used to produce mind-altering drugs—however efficiently done?
3. Is there a difference between "effectiveness" and "efficiency" in the use of national resources?
4. What is your concept of progress?
   a. Do *social* values and goals enter in?
   b. Is social progress feasible without an individual motivation to evolve?
   c. What is the lesson of Russia's policy toward individual progress?
5. Are there absolute social values? *Absolute* personal values?
   a. If so, have we lost touch with them? How can we return them?

b. If not, what is the likely new set of values and where will they come from?

c. What is the *purpose* of having values?

SELECTED READINGS

Bell, Daniel, and Irvin Kristol. *Capitalism Today.* New York: Mentor Books, 1970.

Bennett, J. C., H. R. Bowen, W. A. Brown, and G. B. Oxnam. *Christian Values and Economic Life.* New York: Harper Brothers, 1953.

Chamberlain, N. W. *The Place of Business in America's Future.* New York: Basic Books, 1973.

———. *The Limits of Corporate Responsibility.* New York: Basic Books, 1973.

Donaldson, Thomas and Patricia H. Werhane. *Ethical Issues in Business.* Englewood Cliffs, N.J.: Prentice-Hall, 1979.

Fiselius, Arne, and Sam Nilsson, (eds.). *The Place of Value in a World of Facts.* New York: Wiley-Interscience, 1970.

Petit, T. A. *The Moral Crisis in Management.* New York: McGraw-Hill, 1967.

Tawney, R. H. *Equality.* London: Geo. Allen & Unwin, 1952.

Van Dam, C., and L. Stallaert. *Trends in Business Ethics.* Boston: Martinus Nijhoff, 1978.

Chapter 5

Corporate Social Responsibility
vs.
Socialism

This chapter explores the idea that the businessman is creating socialism in America by his lack of social responsibility. If you think business is not doing so, give me a few minutes, and we will see where we end up. In order to demonstrate that this is a serious proposition, I wish to quote from the conservative economist, Milton Friedman; he has intermittently been an advisor to various governments and is a Nobel prize winner. He said the following in an interview with *Business and Society Review* (Spring 1972): "If this country becomes a collective socialist country, I don't believe it will be because socialists will win at the ballot box. It will be because of wage and price controls." He added that if you seriously control prices, you have to ration goods and you have to allocate labor. All businessmen profess to be free enterprisers, he said, "however, the truth of the matter is that the biggest enemies of free enterprise are businessmen. And they have always been."

Now that is about as strong a statement of the orientation for this discussion that I could find, and obviously having found it from an economist who believes in private enterprise, it is a bit more striking. (I hesitate to tell you what he would do in order to recreate free enterprise, because you might stop reading Milton Friedman afterwards. It includes eliminating all tariffs, thus letting textiles come in from anywhere in the world, breaking up the large corporations and conglomerates, taxing earnings not declared as dividends, taxing excess profits, and so on.)

He also says, however, "There is nothing that would in fact destroy the private enterprise system more than a real acceptance of a social responsibility doctrine. A businessman is supposed to make profit for his stockholders and that is all." Friedman would design the system so that this is *all* business could do—establish a purely competitive system, strictly according to the classical system in which there would be full information in the market, no possibility of monopoly, taxation of all windfall profits, and so forth. He is careful to *footnote* that business behavior should be within the "ethical mores" of the society where it operates.

His system is internally consistent; it is also irrelevant. We have rejected it for 200 years, and we are not going to adopt it now. The question, therefore, is *how* do you operate in the imperfect system that we have and by what criteria? Our reply to date has been inadequate, which is why the system remains under attack, with the result that the Western world is moving toward socialism—some say even totalitarianism.

The first time I heard the prediction that we would have socialism was from my economics professor at Davidson College. (He was a little to the right of Milton Friedman.) He said, "In 25 years we will swing to the left and become a socialist country, and then it will start swinging in the other direction." He was a little premature. That was about 40 years ago, now, and we will haven't quite made it to socialism. Now it is not clear whether we're moving left or right.

A similar prediction was made in 1949 by Joseph Schumpeter, a Harvard professor, in his book on *Capitalism, Socialism, and Democracy*. He argued that business would not be able to solve its own problems and would turn to government for assistance, that business would get so bureaucratic it would lose its entrepreneurship, and that it would be faced with unions which were constantly insisting on more. In order to solve the wage/price spiral, government would get deeper into the problems of business and labor relations. If wars occurred, although he didn't predict them, inflation would accelerate and this would bring on even more governmental controls. He predicted socialism before 1980.

Further, Schumpeter argued, only a capitalist country could afford socialism. To try to adopt socialism before a country has had capitalism is silly. It's like a little country in Central America I heard about which had just adopted a very extensive social welfare program on the advice of a French socioeconomist who had been asked to design their social welfare program. When he was told that his entire program had passed the legislature, he said, "I am so happy; the French government said they couldn't afford it." Schumpeter thought the same in principle. You can't afford socialism until you are rich.

But when capitalism cannot solve the problems that arise, business will turn to government, and government will think it can afford socialism. By "affording it" Schumpeter did not mean that it would be "good." He simply meant that the pain wouldn't be all that much and we would accept it. That's the same thing Friedman is saying: business is willing to accept wage and price control because it cannot solve the problems of unemployment and inflation, or is unwilling to, and the cost of letting the government do it isn't all that much.

It isn't just wage and price control I want to talk about. Rather, it is a substantial shift in the institutions of our system, altering the ethical bases of behavior for the corporation and for management.

As we discussed earlier, capitalism is itself an ethical system, and it assumes a certain ethical behavior by the individuals operating within it. We have considered in addition, the criteria by which conduct is judged—in terms of justice in dealing with people, equity, truth, freedom, virtue, and so on. But how are they expressed? According to Adam Smith and Milton Friedman, they should be built into the design of the whole society, so that business *can* simply pursue profits and *thereby* serve society. The capitalist system ought to be designed, they say, so that *all* of the ethical constraints are *in* it: it would be impossible for business to make profits illegally or unethically. Of course, there is no way to design a *free* system so that all individual choices will *have* to be ethical. Our past efforts to do so broke down—partly because the enemy is the businessman himself. He doesn't want to operate that way. Airlines have fought deregulation; textiles want to reduce foreign competition (fair or not); the list is endless. Nobody *really* wants to face strong competition, though all assert their support for a competitive society. I once had a colleague—a conservative economist who espoused the virtues of free enterprise—who was offered a promotion by another university, but without tenure. He wanted to accept, but wanted tenure immediately whereas the university wanted to wait a year. I asked him what happened to his ideas of risk-taking enterprise. He replied, "that is good for the rest of society, but not for me; I want security." Nearly everybody tries to build protective walls around themselves—with or without government help!

How do we induce business to operate according to the ethics of the system? The accompanying diagram shows the potential inputs into a company which affect its behavior and those affected by it. One complaint heard these days is that there seem to be inadequate channels for inputs into management decisions, and for those affected to respond. How, for example, do the stockholders impose any ethical criteria on management? Friedman says they don't; they shouldn't; and if they could, they wouldn't want to, for all they are interested in is dividends. If you give them enough return they will shut up and go home, and leave management to do what it wants. We hear of dissident minority stockholders trying to impose ethical criteria on management on such matters as minority hiring of blacks, activities abroad, discrimination against women, product safety, pollution, and so on. But how the stockholder's input is to be made is still an open question. Who are the stockholders who should be heard, and how should their voice be translated into action?

Other parts of society are also concerned—namely, the consumers. What kind of input does the consumer have into business decisions? Why do we need a government office of consumer affairs? Obviously to increase the voice of the consumer—to raise quality and achieve fair prices. Do companies actually take lower profits in order to price their goods "fairly"? Is pricing done for ethical reasons, as compared to profit? Or will a company *use* profits in order to conduct an

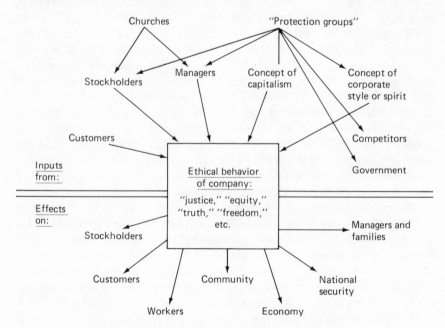

Figure 5-1. Social responsibility inputs and outputs.

ethically desirable program? In support for education, for example, charitable contributions are a charge against profits: this is an ethically oriented action, presumably, producing equity and justice. To the extent that business has been doing such things, it has already recognized that there are some ethical inducements or constraints on the company which are not built directly into Capitalism, but are somehow expected in a community. The company might not get any direct return for such actions. It can't possibly compute what business return will derive from a specific community contribution.

There are other ethical constraints which business is willing to meet, even at a cost in profits. For example, even if the child labor laws were repealed, I don't think there are many companies that would go back to taking advantage of children. When such actions are discovered, we count those people as "unscrupulous," meaning without (ethical) scruples and seeking to make money out of anything.

Would tobacco companies go into marijuana if it became legal to smoke it? How does the community express their dislike for such a result, assuming it disapproved? You might ask: If business is part of a community, isn't it just as important for that business to see that it makes profit, to stay healthy, as it is to see that its employees get to the doctor once a year to stay healthy? Only if in both cases you have done it by acceptable means. If you send the worker to a quack, although your intentions are good, you harm him. If you make profits by means in which the community does not agree are acceptable, you destroy the business system, which is exactly what is happening in some cases. I'm not saying that the entire business world is unethical today. What *has* happened is that not all business is making sure to gain their profits by wholly ethical ways—ways that are accepted by the society. Is the society always right? No, business does not have to assume that "society" is always right. But to alter that view, business must participate in society and express its views publicly; otherwise, society will change the *system*, probably toward socialism. It is not enough merely to assert that "the business of business is business." That is beautifully trite. It says nothing and everything at the same time. It says, "I can't think of any other way to describe it, except by its own name." That is a very poor stance for business, but it is often said. J. Paul Getty said, "If a man hasn't got business, what has he got?" If this is all that business can say, it will never be able to think through the problem. It is as though business sees society as the opposition. If there is anything I have been trying to say it is this: "Stop seeing critics as being on the *other* side of the table." The problems which are being raised *do* exist. If you want to persuade the others to see the problem in a different light, don't attack them or even defend your own actions. Recognize the problem, instead, and then seek to analyze it together to reach an acceptable solution. If a free system is to remain, business must see *both* the consumer and society as collaborators—not as competitors, or the enemy. The society was *not* constructed for business, but the other way around. Business must serve the ends of society, and it must do so by acceptable means, or either the *system* or business' role in it will be changed.

I was talking to one of the officials of my University the other day on a matter on which he had opposed some of us in the Business School. I said, "You stupid guy, you don't know enough about this problem to recognize even what it is." That's what I told him, right? No! I figuratively walked around the desk, got on his side, and said, "We have a problem. Let's look at it." We started taking it apart, and the more we took it apart, the more nuances there were in the thing. The more I accepted his viewpoint, the more I was able to push some of my own in. We didn't hack each other apart.

If business wants to come out swinging, it is going to hit itself on the head, because the problems are real and itself is at the center. "Profit is not a four-letter word," the statement goes. Nobody said it was!—at least nobody you want to listen to. Such a person already has his mind encased, if he thinks that profit is bad. Some of us don't think it is a four-letter word—but we still recognize that there are problems. Even if you and I *didn't* think that business is under pressure, there are enough polls to give us pause in our view.

Right now, I am trying to focus on the fact that if you want to be influential in persuading society to see things in a different light than it does, business had better recognize that there *are* some fundamental problems. How different GM would have been if it had publicly thanked Ralph Nader for what he did in publicizing the defects in the Corvair, and gone hand–in–hand with him to satisfy the consumer! Actually, I don't think they could have boosted Nader anymore than they did. They might have pulled his teeth by saying, "Yes, we did slip here . . .", if it was true. The record has never finally come out on the Corvair, as far as I know, and it is an error in itself not to have the full record out on it. GM could have taken the initiative, saying, "Look how many cars we have pulled back." Since they later *had* to do so, obviously there was a problem. There are problems of design, safety, future investment, employment, profits, and so on. *Not* to recognize this and combat it, focusing on the problem, is the real error in my view.

GM's attack on Nader gave more credence to Nader's views than he could produce from the evidence. It's true companies are not perfect all the time, and no one can expect perfection. The problem is in *not* making this clear to begin with—that there will be some difficulties—and standing ready at any time to make corrections. A few of the companies have come up with the response, "We have a Vice President at the phone: dial 800-000-0000 to get your problems solved." That's a move in the direction of consumer satisfaction, true, but it is important to note how it occurred to companies to do so. They did so not in anticipation of problems, but only after consumer complaints threatened to bring in the government. The lack of company initiative was noted in a 1975 report by the Business Roundtable on "Ethics and Business Leadership." Every problem left unresolved by business leaders is going to be resolved by somebody else. Do "they" know better? Not necessarily, but they are part of any resolution, and unless "they" and business work together, the resolution will move toward more government interference. Every time a problem is resolved by Congress or the Executive or a regulatory agency, we are one step closer to socialism. Take heed of the fact that it has recently been proposed that the oil companies be nationalized.

There are precious few significant social problems that business has handled on its own initiative. At every junction, in the area of ethical problems and social responsibility—justice, truth, or whatever else—business has said, "We cannot handle it. Let the government do it." Take truth in lending, truth in advertising, truth in packaging. Where is the resolution for these issues? You can say that the laws shouldn't have been passed. You can say that the laws are too constraining, and that they are unjust, but you have further to prove there was *no* problem in the first place. If there was a problem, we need to know why business didn't handle it.

I agree that not all businesses were acting in violation of the purposes of these laws. A lot of consumer products are given black eyes by the implications of truth in packaging legislation. There is also the problem that no one business can command ethical behavior on the part of another. Each segment, however, of industry or business could promulgate ethical rules and enforce them. Doctors have ethical rules; dentists have ethical rules. They are enforced to the letter, right? No! O.K., now we are beginning to get to the problem. Business has an even tougher time gaining the right to form its own rules because it is not seen as having a "professional dedication." Bankers have a "Banker's Association," but is there a code of ethics for bankers? Implied? How? Imposed how? By law! You see, anytime we get to the problem of behavior, we get back to the role of government. In order to enforce something, even a code which could be agreed on in a given segment of industry or finance, we turn to government for enforcement—even for the *definition* of what is agreed on!

If business thinks that these laws or rules are not as they should be, it has the opportunity and the *right* to persuade society of its view. But if it asserts a right to decide merely by *power*—that is, "I have the power to make this decision and therefore I do it"—it has not persuaded society of the *rightness* of its position. Business may be right, but increasingly, as the society or *groups* within the society gain strength, they will change the rules because they can, even if they are "wrong."

The question before us is how can business move to reduce such governmental interferences—or is socialism in fact inevitable? Friedman argues that when business starts playing around with social responsibility and telling each other what to do, all that results is a mucked up system. He says, "Let government set the *rules* and let business just be efficient in seeking profits." He argues that if we continue the way we are now, we will end up with socialism.

These issues are real. They are going to have to be given answers. Business can answer them itself; that is one possibility! By following certain ethical behavior, it can cut the problem off at the pass. Or, it can let the government start to provide answers and then argue with it. Or, it can give up and say, "The hell with it; whatever the government does, I will live with, as long as everyone else has to." I've heard many businessmen say that, given the condition that the rules would be the same for all. But business doesn't have to be that passive. Managers have a vote; they have an argument; and they have some powers of persuasion.

There are some people who think business has too much power vis-à-vis government already, keeping government from doing things it should do to control business or help society. They want to establish justice, equity, truth, virtue, freedom, and so forth—and force business to do so, too, through government constraints. But business can set its own rules. For example, J. Ervin Miller of Cummins Engine has recently restated his policy of 100% adherence to honesty, even if the company loses profits—even if it hurts. Now that is a statement of self-policing. I don't know what the impact of that is on his executives. I don't even know what 100% honesty means in selling an engine—different things to different salesmen on the line, I am sure. What if you go broke being 100% honest when you could have profits being 60% honest? Well, if the customer learns you are partially dishonest, you'll probably *not* profit, in the long run at least. It seems to me better to pass all relevant information to the customer and treat him fairly—that is, honestly. Capitalism and free enterprise include the right to *fail* as well as to succeed. And success is not to be achieved at another's expense—certainly not at the price of deceiving the customer, who is supposed to be *served*.

The recent exposure of insurance companies selling multiple health and medical policies to elderly persons who neither need nor can afford them reveals that there are companies in industry that are not policing themselves, even though there is substantial policing by state governments. When the consumer pays for something he does not want and, because of overlapping coverage, should not get, this accelerates the trend toward national health insurance. If the legal profession doesn't police itself, we are going to have two nationalized professions: legal and medical. I would much prefer them to police themselves—even just follow the ethics they say they have! When I say they don't follow their own rules, I mean they have a sufficient number not doing so to spoil the barrel for all. If they don't police themselves, national regulation is likely, and the results are not going to be very helpful. I recognize that one company's initiative is difficult. As a manager told me once: "Pollution regulations are going to cost the furniture industry millions of dollars. I live in a town that is full of furniture plants and I'd like to have the air cleaned up as much as anybody else. But if any one company on their own decided to clean up their stacks, it would cost them several million dollars. Right away they would be uncompetitive and they would be gone. You have to have some regulation so everybody can be equal."

O.K., so the *individual* company can't take the initiative by itself. But all could do so together. Who should bear the competitive loss in following ethical or socially acceptable behavior? Can a company risk such losses? or is it going to be honest no matter what others do? Suppose one is honest and his profits drop 2% compared to his competitors, what is going to happen? Some managers assert he will eventually go out of business. Conversely, if business, guided by a profit motive, is willing to make tradeoffs against all ethical criteria in order to raise profits, then it *is going* to be heavily regulated. Of course, tradeoffs are necessary. Even the public makes tradeoffs against ethics or social goals in order to have jobs. For example, recent layoffs in steel have caused labor to seek relaxation of pollution requirements. Alaskans fought to have the pipeline rather than a cleaner environment. And if you turned out all of the lights in Chapel Hill for a week, our concerned populace would be a little more liberal about polluting energy sources.

It is nonetheless important that such tradeoffs be made by those who are affected, and on the basis of adequate information. It is important that we don't make judgments for the *other* fellow—only for ourselves, however large our group is. I am perfectly willing for the people in Florida, who are the ones affected by it, to decide whether or not they are for a canal or airport and where each should be located. But I don't think *we* have the right to tell people in the West to destroy their community in order to have air conditioning or heating in New York. I admit it's a tough question! The problem rests in who bears the burdens and who benefits—just as we in Chapel Hill told the rural residents of Cane Creek that they should be flooded out of their homes and farmland to provide water for the University and its students. They didn't accept that tradeoff. This is getting at the right of groups in society to rule themselves. Occasionally, some people will have to give up their individual rights for the welfare of all people. That is why such matters are put before the government to decide—not the water company.

Taking another illustration, if a company produces a dress out of fabric, and one woman buys it to wear for a year and then throw it away, while another woman has bought the same dress but is on low income and expects that fabric to wear for five years—how much quality should be built into that fabric? I see no specific requirement for quality to be built in at all. All you have responsibility to do is tell the truth about the wearability. Neither customer may even ask you the question: sometimes they don't know enough to ask, or even how to ask, "is this a good piece of goods?" "Yes," you say, "it is a good piece of goods." "Is it good for five years?" "That depends on how you are going to wear it. Are you going to hang it in your closet and wear it once a week? Or are you going to wear it everyday? Normal wear expectations of this product are three years (three months, whatever it is) . . . ." Products are not generally sold that way. That much information is not generally given. And since it isn't, the woman who wanted to wear it for five years could conclude, "This company is bad. They didn't make me a fabric that lasted five years." Business gets a black eye for something that should not have been expected; therefore all relevant information should be given to the customer to begin with.

Consider the situation an insurance salesman posed me: We have an obligation to tell the truth, so let's say I must explain an insurance claim to a widow with children. Her husband had a $100,000 policy, and the death certificate said her husband died in an airplane crash. We go back and find out he decided to go to the airport and take some flying lessons. It is clearly stated, not in legal terms but in layman's terms, that you have to be on a regularly scheduled airline to collect in case of death in an air crash. How do I explain this to the wife? That provision happens to be in my own policy. It's all right; it is there, and as far as it goes it is at least not a tricky provision. It should be straightforwardly understood. But if the widow considers the insurance company to be biased, she will have to take her lawyer's advice on it. He will simply have to corroborate that it is both legally and ethically appropriate and that the husband violated the policy. You can't violate your company policy in order to take care of her ignorance; that responsibility for explanation and proper behavior devolved on her husband, and he should have protected her. The point is to make *him* sufficiently aware of the limitations; then it becomes his responsibility to inform his family. You don't have to assume *his* responsibility. But without fulfilling your own responsibility, greater governmental regulation is inevitable.

DISCUSSION QUESTIONS

1. Why is it that businessmen were not averse to wage and price controls in the inflationary conditions of the early 1970s?
   a. Can they be imposed equitably?
   b. If not, should they ever be imposed?
2. What has been the attitude of business toward the control's imposed by government over business operations?
   a. Should business have taken this position? Why? Why not?
   b. What impression have these positions made on the society?
3. Why do polls continue to report low public confidence in business and government institutions and leadership?
4. Is government regulation the same thing as socialism?
   a. What is the essence of socialism?
   b. How far is the U.S. away from adopting it?
   c. If it comes, will it come by sectors through increasing control or nationalization? Which sectors?
   d. Or will it come through national planning?—or through election of socialist representations?
5. What can business do to halt or counter such possibilities?
   a. Individually?
   b. Collectively?

SELECTED READINGS

Beauchamp, T. L., and N. E. Bowie. *Ethical Theory and Business.* Englewood Cliffs, N.J.: Prentice-Hall, 1979, Chap. 3.
Chamberlain, John. *The Roots of Capitalism.* Indianapolis: Liberty Press, 1976.

Chamberlain, N. W. *The Place of Business in American's Future*. New York: Basic Books, 1973.

Novak, Michael. *The American Vision*. Washington, D.C.: American Enterprise Institute, 1978.

Revel, J. F. *The Totalitarian Temptation*. Garden City, N.Y.: Doubleday, 1977.

Shonfield, A. *Modern Capitalism*. Fair Lawn, N.J.: Oxford University Press, 1965.

Van Dam, Cees, and Lund Stallaert. *Trends in Business Ethics*. Boston: Martinus Nijhoff, 1978.

Walton, C. C. *Corporate Social Responsibilities*. Belmont, Cal.: Wadsworth Publishing Co., 1967.

Chapter 6

Business a Game?

The purpose of this discussion is to examine the question of whether or not business is a game, and if so, whether it should follow certain rules, as games do. If business is not a game, is it a unique function in the society, with its own unique set of rules? Or is business more like war, abiding by the rules of war—if there are any? Alternatively, is business a part of life and therefore must abide by the rules applicable to life in general? Is it possible there are *no* rules at all? Once we have examined these questions we will turn to a discussion of who sets the rules and what the specific rules for business should be. I do not wish to make a forced comparison. I think you will find the exercise useful in helping to see the nature of business and what is expected of it by society.

CHARACTERISTICS OF GAMES AND A GAME

Games in general have certain characteristics and purposes in society. Specific games have specific characteristics and objectives. What are the characteristics and purposes of games in general? First, as to purposes, games are introduced into life for the purpose of pure "play," permitting diversion and creating certain types of pleasure. Games also have the purpose of recreation, for both the body and the mind. They are also intended to provide certain learning experiences in preparation for future roles. Said Fraser, in his *Words on Wellington*, "The battle of Waterloo was won on the playing fields of Eton." Games are also meant to demonstrate the achievement of certain standards of discipline or prowess. Games in some societies are played to replicate social behavior or social hierarchy, reinforcing and stabilizing the social structure. You may think of other purposes of games in a society, but this is enough to get us started in our discussion.

Now, let's characterize games. What are they made of? Players, obviously, but what else? A definition of the contest. Volunary entry. Rules. Strategy and tactics. There also has to be an uncertainty as to outcome, and a period which determines the beginning and end of play. Spectators? Well, not all games involve spectators and some such as poker, discourage them. Where the entertainment of spectators *is* a feature of the game, it is likely to be considered by many as "a business"—and therein lies the heart of our discussion.

Different configurations of each of these characteristics leads to different kinds of games. Not all games have a set number of players, being open-ended as to the number who can participate; others, of course, are quite fixed in that regard. The nature of the contest in some games is purely competitive: in others it is based on considerable cooperation, such as where team efforts are required. All games, however, are characterized by voluntarism; that is, the players enter the game voluntarily. Otherwise, it is not a game! This does not mean that persuasion is wholly absent from the matter of who will play and when, but contests in which the actors are under duress—such as the Christians in the Roman Coliseum—hardly constitute a game. At least the Christians were not playing!

The objective of any individual or group entering a game is generally to win the game, but this objective is constrained by the desire to play the game again. Therefore, behavior is guided by the desire of both parties to induce the other to agree voluntarily to future games. Certain strategies and tactics are employed during the game in order to win, and the players who know the better strategies and can exercise them through the most efficient tactics are most likely to win—though chance also plays a part in many games.

Consequently, all games are characterized by uncertainty. The players usually do not know beforehand the outcome of the game or who is going to win. If they *do* know with a high degree of certainty that one player will win, as in a contest, for example, between a professional and an amateur, there is still some uncertainty about how much the one is going to win over the other. The contest is then an exercise in improving against expectations. It is still a game, and it will still be played. Also, there is always the chance that expectations can be completely reversed.

Although there is uncertainty in a game, there is no risk for the players. That is, there is no risk of damaging loss if the contest is a pure game. Players may add risk to any game by speculating on the outcome, but this is not a necessary part of the game. It then becomes a game mixed with risk taking, through the wagering of money or other material goods, and it gets called a "game of chance"— or gambling, where the skill element is different from pure games.

For games to be played so that the outcome is clear, and so the players will return to play again, there must be agreed-upon rules for playing. These rules may be set by the players as they enter the game (remember the long negotiations over chess rules between Fisher and Spassky?); they may be set by tradition in a given community; or they may be set quite formally by a commission acting at the national or international levels. Whatever the rules are, they should be known fully to all players, and there should be no changes in the rules *during* the play. (There are games in which one of the rules is that the rules are changed, given certain events, and the Japanese game of "Go" often involves changes in procedures which have an effect on the outcome.) Finally, these rules have to be followed if there is to *be* a game, and penalties imposed when the rules are *not* followed. If "winning" becomes more important than playing the game, the rules are likely to be broken, and eventually the game will be altered. For example, the fastest woman runner in the 1979 New York marathon reportedly was uninterested in competing in the Olympics because of the allegedly pervasive illegal use of anabolic steroids by women to make them stronger (more manly). "Russia and other Eastern European countries will do anything to win the gold medal," she said, since some countries view Olympic results as evidence of national and ideological superiority. This, of course, is a perversion of the purpose of the Olympic games.

In games, there is also a scoring procedure which permits players to know how they are progressing in the contest and eventually to determine who is the winner, if any. This scoring is nothing but a set of tallies which should not be confused with the game itself, nor even with its purpose.

There is a referee, umpire, or other means for determining whether the rules are complied with and for settling disputes over particular plays. In some games, of course, the players themselves are the referees. Tennis is called a "gentlemen's game," and is reputed to be a game in which absolute honesty can be attributed to each of the players: if a player calls a ball "out," it *was* in fact out! For those of you who are golfers, as I am, it is interesting to note that golf is not called a "gentlemen's game"—probably because scoring is sometimes characterized by the expression, "put me down for a bogey," which often means that the score was higher. In most games, however, the referees are supposed to be separate from the players and wholly objective. They are frequently seen as considerably biased—in favor of the opponents of your team—but since they are seen in the same light by the opponent's supporters, it is likely that they are, on the whole, relatively unbiased and fair—that is, when they are not "blind."

Finally, there is a known time period for most games, though not all, such as baseball, tennis, cricket, or the Japanese game of "Go." The termination of a game is sometimes tied to the passage of a specific number of minutes or periods; in others, to the amassing of a particular score; and in still others to a combination of the two. All that is required is that the termination procedure be known to all parties and accepted by them prior to play.

There are other characteristics of games worth noting, such as complex equipment which raises the costs of playing and reduces the number who can participate in the game. The cost of swimming pools, for example, may prevent certain people from becoming swimmers. In other cases, such as touch football, the absence of protective equipment has set the rules of the game.

As we shall see later, all of these characteristics are applicable to business, though they are not expressed in precisely the same way. Before we get to that discussion, however, let us stop to examine the nature of war.

WAR AS A GAME

War has often been characterized as a game. It is worth pursuing the similarities and differences, because business has often been described as war. This exercise in comparison should help clarify the role of rules and how they are set.

The purposes of war in general have historically encompassed a wide range, including the spread or perpetuation of religious views, the alteration of power relationships, pure tests of strength, acquisition of wealth, and a type of "play" between societies which has taken on more of a ritual character than that of outright destruction.

Wars have also been used as a means of teaching young men the values of fortitude, courage, and strength, along with loyalty and sacrifice. These multiple purposes run parallel to some of the purposes of games, but they are distinct enough to force us to conclude that war and games are by no means identical in purpose.

As in *some* games, the number of players in war can be indefinite, and the contest requires both competitive and cooperative acts on the part of the various players.

In contrast to games, however, wars are not always fought under voluntarism. Either one or both of the nations or groups involved may consider that they were left no choice by the acts of the other. The soldiers may have been conscripted rather than permitted to volunteer for service. Wars, therefore, are much more serious than games—as shown also in the objective of any particular war.

The objective of a nation engaging in war is to win it, as in playing a game. With war, however, there can be no clear determination about when the war has been won. There have been wars of annihilation in which the war was not said to be won until the enemy was not only vanquished but eliminated. Wars of annihilation, in Old Testament history, were said to be ordered by God at the hands of the Israelites, with only the young virgins to be spared the sword. Such wars were, of course, directed at removing the enemy from the land so that the Israelites could occupy it. No modern wars among "civilized" countries have been wars of annihilation—although the war in Cambodia in 1979 came close, if press reports were accurate.

In the main, the objective of any given war is to achieve limited goals ranging from absolute surrender to a new accommodation among the contestants. Here we find a clear distinction between war and games, since no game has as an objective the elimination of the opponent—to annihilate him or eliminate his interest in playing the game in the future. In modern war, at least, no party would enter the war with the *purpose* of anticipating a subsequent war.

Wars, like games, require strategy and tactics, and there is considerable uncertainty as to the outcome. In war, there is considerable risk to all parties involved, simply because the costs of engaging in war are substantial. Even if the war is won, the costs to the victor may not be offset by the spoils. If one adds to the cost what the conduct of the war does to the social fabric and the moral fiber of both the conquered and conquering people, it should be clear from an ethical standpoint that there are no winners in wars at all. A basic distinction, then, between wars and games, is that wars are not acts of recreation, as are games, but are destructive of many facets of life.

Despite the apparent "no holds barred" approach to war, in fact, wars are conducted by various rules. There are rules concerning the treatment of prisoners, and rules about the tactics and equipment permissible in the conduct of a war. Mustard gas was prohibited in World War I because of its uncontrolled effects. Similarly, nerve gas and biological warfare were prohibited in World War II because of the potential effects on noncombatants and the tendency to annihilate the opponent—as well as the fact that the user himself might be damaged. There are also rules about the acceptable involvement of noncombatants and about damage done to historical landmarks. Of course, not all combatants always abide by the rules, but that does not mean that rules are nonexistent. In whatever social arrangement one finds rules, one will also find that they are sometimes broken. The mere breaking does not prove the absence of rules; rather, there must *be* rules for them to be "broken."

Wars have other similarities to games. Frequently, a score is kept— as was the case in the Vietnam War, when the Pentagon periodically announced "body counts" in an effort to demonstrate that the U.S. was winning on the basis of the numbers of soldiers killed on each side. Similar scores were kept for the number of planes shot down, bridges destroyed, supply lines disrupted, and so forth. (The impact of such scorekeeping on war strategy leads into quite another discussion. For example, it was cited at the time as leading to a "dehumanization" of the war by giving the impression that only "bodies" were killed rather than people or human beings.) Other means of keeping score include the land area occupied and the number of battles "won." Of course, none of this scorekeeping directly determines who wins the war—as we have found to our sorrow in Vietnam. However, it is obvious that if one side is winning by all of the *relevant* scores— and the score is being kept accurately—it is highly likely that the enemy will eventually be forced in surrender negotiations.

Given the fact that there are rules of war, one would expect that referees would be needed. In fact they do exist, but in quite a different form than in games. The public itself acts as a referee in war. This was the intention of certain anti-Vietnam War protesters when they displayed pictures of alleged bombings of citizen targets and the effects of fire-bombing with napalm: to provoke the U.S. public to constitute itself as a referee on the particular tactics or strategies employed. At the end of a war, the winner may constitute himself as a referee, punishing the loser for violations of the rules of war—as was done in the Nuremberg Trials after World War II. Similar judgments are passed on defeated leaders of civil wars in many countries today. The judgment is not directed at the fact that they lost, but at the way in which they conducted the war.

Unlike games, wars do not have any period for their termination, and may go on for many years—as did the Thirty Years War in Europe. Finally, as with games, the cost of equipment for war will limit those who can participate and alter the way in which the war can be fought.

In sum, we find that wars have many of the characteristics of games, including rules and a kind of a refereeing that takes place, during and after a given war. The greatest distinction, perhaps, is that wars are fought to eliminate the competitor's ability to play.

BUSINESS: WAR OR GAME?

We can now turn to the question of whether business is a game or war. If we compare the characteristics of business to those of games and war, we will find numerous similarities, especially where wars and games are themselves similar. For example, the purpose of business in the society is the creation of goods and services through the application of man's mind and body to natural resources. Games are the reverse, in a sense, having as their purpose the recreation of the mind and body, and *using* for this purpose the products of business or the bounty of nature. Business is not "play" for the society as a whole—but an individual may certainly consider business activities as "play" to him or her. It could be so stimulating and enjoyable as to be recreative in itself. Like games, business provides an opportunity for growth on the part of both the individual and the social groups involved. And, like games and war, it provides a test of skills—in meeting the demands of consumers in the most efficient manner—or a test of power, if the market is quasi-monopolistic.

The numbers of players in any business contest is indefinite, unless some are precluded by governmental rules or by the power or cost situation at the time. In conducting business, the contestants must both compete and cooperate, just as they must in war and games. Participation in business, as in games, is voluntary; there *are* other ways of earning a living.

The vocabulary of game-playing is often employed as a means of defining the objective of business, as in "winning." At other times, the objective is described as "survival"—the opposite being annihilation. Thus, the words that are used to define business objectives are similar to those for both war and games. Terms such as "strategy," "tactics," or "game plan" are also employed to illustrate the methods of doing business.

Business is faced with uncertainty—although managers would

dearly like to remove it. It is no more possible to remove uncertainty from business, however, than it is from games or war, since the entire society, in all of its parts, continually faces uncertainty. Business also faces risks, some of which it can reduce or insure against, placing itself somewhere between a game player (with no risks) and a warrior (who risks everything.) Far from seeking risks, however, business generally seeks to avoid risks, and managers are best characterized as risk-averters rather than risk-takers. In between are entrepreneurs and so-called "free enterprisers," who are predominantly risk-assumers. If business actually *sought* out risks, they would be acting like speculators, seeking to gain on the differential expectations about the likelihood of particular events. But businesses deny that they are speculators—and in the main they are not. A few businessmen may be "high-rollers" or gamblers—even with their own companies—but few managers can afford to act in this way with a company that is owned by others.

For the present discussion, the most important point is that business is subject to rules—just as games and war. To be useful to society, business must be conducted in such a way that it produces the goods demanded by society and *does so under conditions and by procedures which are acceptable to the society.* The mere fact of "winning" is not enough; the profits must be earned in an acceptable fashion. This acceptability implies the existence of acceptable *patterns of conduct*, derived from following the rules. Under capitalism, as we regarded it in the first sessions, the rules of behavior for business were fairly explicit and included a specific type of competition—described as "atomistic"—conducted within a free market. These rules clearly affect the method of keeping score, as well as satisfaction with the score achieved.

The score for a company is profits and losses. I hesitate to mention losses, but losses do occur and they are part of the score-keeping. They may or may not be a *result* of actions by the company or its managers, but they constitute, nevertheless, the company's score. There is an interesting characterization of profits and losses in annual reports which is similar to that used by students in describing their grades. Profits are said to be "earned" or "made," while losses are merely "sustained"—just as a student will say "I *made* an A," but "the prof *gave* me a D."

In fact, profits are frequently the result of general business conditons; they may even, at times, be purely paper profits, as in the case of inflated inventory values. Neither profits nor losses are strictly attributable to management capabilities or activities, though they are used to measure management "performance." The score in business is frequently more attributable to chance than it is to performance of the players. This being the case, a focusing on score as though it were the *purpose* of business is likely to warp the conduct of business and lead to violations of the rules.

There are rules; therefore, there must be referees. As in some games, the referees in business are often the players themselves. There are also external rule-setters and enforcers—the government and the courts. We are most concerned here with self-imposed rules and self-refereeing, as it were, although we'll also have to consider legal constraints and surveillance.

Business activities, unlike wars or games, are not necessarily terminated at any time. They may be indefinite, lasting over several generations. However, one could visualize a given contract as equivalent to a "play" within a game, or similar to a battle within a war.

A final similarity to both games and war is that the nature of the equipment involved in business affects those who are able to participate and the way in which the activities are conducted. The equipment, for example, used in service industries is radically different from that in high-technology operations.

Despite its similarities to war and games, business is a unique activity within society. Is it closer, perhaps, to life itself? If so, what are the rules, if any?

LIFE AS A GAME

Let's look at life itself as a game, noting the distinctions, and then see where there is a fit between business and life.

As we discussed in the first session, the purpose of life, at least within the Western world and within the Judeo-Christian tradition, is to glorify God through the individual's perfecting himself. This is expressed by a person's effort to be creative and to reach higher levels of understanding and unity with God. Such creativity may be on a different plane, but it is not different in concept from that required in business or games. Life is certainly not supposed to be devoid of joy; in fact, the process of creation is itself supposed to be joyous, as is the glorification of God. Life, like games, is a process of learning, growing, and testing or tempering. One of the problems in life is to determine precisely which activities should be competitive and which cooperative; these decisions are pretty well made for us by the rules of a game or of war. Life on earth is a period in which we are to prove ourselves, as seen in the way in which we use the talents and opportunities given us.

The players in life are not limited by selection, since all who exist must play the game. Nor is the decision to enter the game voluntary for an individual in this world—though voluntarism may have characterized the individuals who were the instruments of procreation. There is the alternative of suicide, of course, which at least ends *this* life—or this game or battle. However, we consider suicide against the rules. (It's a stricture that is difficult to enforce; but some nations imposed the death penalty for attempting suicide, so all one has to do is attempt suicide and fail in order to succeed.)

As to the objective of any single life, once again we often speak of "winning," although the opponent is frequently some amorphous concept such as "fate," or "the devil," or even ourselves. Depending on one's religious views, the objective of life may be to reach heaven, to produce heaven on earth, to become enlightened, or to achieve personal wealth, power, and prestige. Some people employ a strategy and a set of tactics by which they expect to achieve their objectives. All individuals face uncertainty, however, and bear substantial risks. And unless they are wholly without ethical or moral constraints, all individuals will live their lives by certain rules—though these rules will change as they proceed through their life.

The rules are both general and specific, and they vary from group to group and individual to individual. The sources of rules vary, too: they can be legally imposed, socially set, theologically determined, and individually accepted.

As to the score in life, we seem to find it difficult to decide how that should be counted—other than in material wealth, social prestige, or political power, each *in comparison* with others! Almost all ethical sources of rules indicate that the score is to be counted in terms of socially-oriented works (stewardship) and in acts which are self-effacing (virtuous) and which glorify God (i.e., respond to God's will). In practice, we act more according to the modified version of the saying concerning "The One Great Scorer"—the version which reads—

> When the One Great Scorer comes,
> a mark against your name to choose,
> *He writes not how you played the game,*
> *but did you win or lose!*

That score is quantified in terms of material wealth! Even those with power and prestige have not "won" until they've gained wealth.

The referee in life—the One Great Scorer—is assumed to be someone other than ourselves: God, in other words, called by whatever name we choose. (Though some would argue that there is no "final judgment," and we are accountable *only* to ourselves.) Since we are not absolutely certain of the criteria which He will employ in the final judgment, score-keeping is a continuous task with rules that shift as our perception expands, is clarified, and we come to "see face to face."

Finally, although life in this physical world is finite, we do not know the period for any given life, nor for human life itself, nor for "life after life." Life is in this sense not at all similar to a game.

The only sense in which life might be a game is if God were playing it. If He were, He would be playing it either with man or the Devil. Some religious concepts include the view that God and the Devil are playing a game of chess in which men are pawns with some small capability of individual decision—e.g., to walk around the board on their own or even choose sides—so the outcome is uncertain for the two main players. In such a game, God suffers (or loses) each time an individual goes over to the Devil's side.

If God were playing a game with man himself, it would have to be merely an educational exercise for man, since it would be impossible for him to win. He would only be capable of improving his performance in competition or in cooperation with the Master.

We are now ready to draw a few conclusions—though many more will occur to you on your own:

COMMONALITY OF RULES

In looking at the characteristics of games, war, business, and life, we can discern first that *all* have rules, and second that there is a commonality among some of the rules for each. For example, is there honor in each? Yes, of course. There is sacrifice in each. Loyalty. Fairness. And honesty. There is also duplicity, cheating, lying, and betrayal, of course. At the fundamental level, the rules of behavior for all are the same; where they differ, the rules for life have priority over the rules for each of the others. In fact, if the rules for *life* were adhered to by all, it is conceivable that there would be no war. If only some abided by them, however, any violation of the rules of life by one group might produce war with those who were trying to adhere to the rules.

While we can conclude that business is not strictly a game, nor is it as serious as war, it is an integral part of life and subject to the same rules of behavior. Business in our society, therefore, is subject to moral and ethical constraints. This point is stressed by Dr. Irving

Kristol, in a speech at Stanford University on "Capitalism versus the Economist?"

> To the degree that we fail to appreciate that capitalism involves educating young people to certain standards of what is good, what is proper, what is desirable, until we begin to understand that that is what capitalism is, I think that economists, who at the moment are regarded as the prime defenders of capitalism, will yet end up making capitalism utterly defenseless before its enemies.

If business is a part of life, can the objectives of business be so narrowly defined as profit-seeking? Would society accept the same objective for doctors?—lawyers?—professors?—government officials?—reporters?—scientists?—auditors?—prison guards?—preachers?—professional athletes? What happens to the credibility and acceptability of behavior of individuals in each of these pursuits if they announce that their objective is the maximization of profits? Would spectators be drawn to a professional football game as readily if they knew that players on one side were paying the referee to make all narrow calls in their favor? Would scientists be respected if they were thought to pursue profit over truth? Would the auditing function be believed if auditors were understood to pursue profit over accuracy in their reports? This issue is the basis for a controversy over whether the "Big Eight" auditing firms ought to be also in the business of management consulting with the companies that they audit. Such an arrangement appears to many to be a conflict of interest and to involve the possibility of shading an audit in order to obtain or retain consulting contracts. The medical profession is not without its own loss of credibility, as more and more cases of unnecessary operations, kickbacks from laboratories, and overcharges for Medicaid are reported.

Can business attempt to live by different rules than those expected of the professions? Yes; it can and should, for there *is* a social justification for profits which is tied to the ethical basis of Capitalism as presented in the first sessions. Profits are supposed to be a reward for efficiency—defined as "market efficiency"—which means that the company earning profits has served the consumers better than others, or at least satisfactorily. In turn, this service to consumers supposedly achieves social equity in providing to the consumer what he wants at the lowest possible price. If the rules of the game are flouted by business, this justification for profits in the system becomes invalid.

Does this make business a profession—especially if it sets its own rules? Not really, for a profession is characterized first by services, with income as a *result*; it can even codify discriminatory pricing to clients, based on their ability to pay. No business is permitted to do this. Incidentally, there is a curious twist in the use of words reflecting the monetary expectations—or income orientation—of the various participants in society. The members of a "profession" are not supposed to have income-maximization as their objectve, though many young doctors and lawyers have entered their professions for this reason. Conversely, the word "professional" as distinct from "amateur," applies to someone who *is* seeking to make money out of particular capabilities or situations—as a "professional gambler" or a "professional athlete." The confusion is compounded by the fact that a member of a profession is also often called a professional; and he is expected to do a "professional job," meaning that it meets acceptable standards.

It is difficult to communicate ideas in this field because, with professionalism, objectives and rules get all mixed up. For example, what is the objective of professional football? It is played in Texas and some other areas to entertain the spectators with football and a little sex display. Professional hockey, on the other hand, is serving the spectators with expertise on the ice and a little violence. Professional wrestling is serving the spectators with some acrobatics and quite a bit of hokum. Which of these is most credible? Professional wrestling may be the most credible, since nobody expects it to be a true game or to have precise rules to be followed. The other games have so altered the playing environment that one doubts the credibility of the way in which the game itself is played—that is, how "professional" it is.

RULE SETTING

When this occurs, it is likely that the rules will be changed. A serious question then arises about *who* should change the rules and for what purposes? At the extreme, if one set of players can dictate the rules, then the outcome may itself be dictated—as a gambler may dictate that poker is played so he wins. If the rules are designed solely to make the game more interesting to the spectators, the credibility of the game itself is in jeopardy. To maintain that credibility, a sports commission is frequently appointed—but then one has to consider the criteria by which the commission is setting the rules, and to what end. The game may be changed to equalize the opportunities for winning among the various teams, as is sought through the draft procedures in professional football; or it may be made more complex, or more directed to the development of skill, as in soccer.

When making money becomes the overriding or single objective, the rules are likely to be altered substantially. I am reminded of an occasion in which a senior lawyer was addressing a law forum about the ethics of his profession, and described the following situation:

> A young lawyer, working for a firm, had also on the side been assisting some elderly friends in arranging their estate—as a personal favor, without connection with the firm. He is no longer working with them. He is given the responsibility within the firm to carry out a transaction for a client of the firm that would be substantially to the detriment of his elderly friends. What does he do?

The speaker asked the audience what was the proper resolution of the problem, and with little pause the head of a law firm rose to say the following: "I see no problem at all. The young man should do what he is paid to do." To this the speaker responded, "I thought that our profession had passed somewhat beyond the morals of the oldest profession." Does a monetary (material) objective justify bending the rules and voiding ethical constraints?

The answer to this question helps in determining whether business should be allowed to set its own rules or participate in setting them. Business can hardly be permitted to set its own rules since its form and role originated at the will of society and are justified by its contribution to society. *Society* must set the rules. This is the justification for the "social contract" between business and the rest of the society. But who represents society? And is business itself included within the overall group? Can business be a participant in the making of rules concerning the role and activities of business? If it is, who within business can speak authoritatively and responsibly? Finally, what criteria should be used in representing the interests of business?

In our society, we have not yet provided precise answers to these questions. There continues to be a dialogue on the question of "social responsibility" of business.

Society has various channels for constructing rules of behavior, beginning with the family and going through all of the various institutions within which one participates during this life. The formal channels are those related to the establishment of customs and traditions of behavior as well as legal constraints. Educational institutions, churches, community, and governments, business associations, and state and national governments are involved in addition to the family. Within the professions, quasi-legislative or judicial bodies help form and apply the rules. It is not clear whether these professionally based bodies are doing an adequate job of maintaining adherence to the rules in each of the major professions. If they are not, in the view of the society, then another institution will be used or created to perform this rule-setting and rule-implementing role.

The responsible institution seems to be government. In recent years, there has been an increasing tendency to grant to the Federal Government the responsibility for setting the rules and implementing them, even on behalf of other representative bodies such as state governments and Boards of Education.

The problem this poses is that it reduces the freedom of individuals as well as the freedom of enterprise. True freedom is gained by setting expectations for one's self higher than others set. Otherwise, one is always under the constraint of the expectations of others. Self-government thus begins with self-discipline, which requires in turn self-adherence to the rules and a concern for their formation and application. In the following chapters, we will consider what some of the rules for business must be if its behavior is to become acceptable to society.

DISCUSSION QUESTIONS

1. Is it too forced a comparison to discuss business as a game? Why? What elements are *not* applicable?
2. Is violence a part of the purpose of games?
   a. If so, is there a limit to its expression? What should the limit be?
   b. If not, why is it there?
   c. If not, who should be responsible for its elimination?
3. In business, what is the equivalent of violence in games? How should it be limited or eliminated? By whom?
4. What are the rules for business behavior?
   a. Who should set them?
   b. Can they be codified?
   c. How should they be enforced?
5. Is man a pawn in a cosmic game of life?
   a. If so, what is the purpose of this game?
   b. Who is winning?

SELECTED READINGS

Hodges, L. H. *The Business Conscience.* Englewood Cliffs, N.J.: Prentice-Hall, 1963.

Knight, F. H. *The Ethics of Competition.* New York: Augustus M. Kelly, 1935, Chap. II.

Silk, Leonard and David Vogel. *Ethics and Profits.* New York: Simon & Schuster, 1976.

Chapter 7

Truth, Information Disclosure, and the Right to Lie

Now we can begin to come to grips with the application of some of the values which underlie capitalism and which are supposed to be exemplified in business behavior. These values include justice, honesty, truth, self-respect, stewardship, freedom, equity, respect for privacy, and so forth—as expressed in the four-way path of Rotary, or the 12 parts of the Boy Scout oath. They overlap in their application and even in their concepts. As we have seen earlier, they also sometimes conflict in application to specific situations.

There are no neat solutions to the problem of implementation of values. Each one of us will continue to have to face the problem of how to comply with or fulfill our values in a myriad of different situations. For those of us who would like to have more certainty in life, this is an unfortunate situation. I am reminded of the request by a member of an ethics discussion group in our church some years ago. In a voice of desperation, he asked the pastor, "Can you simply tell me what is right and wrong? Then I will do it." It is not that easy. We should not expect to discover a clear dividing line between right and wrong for each situation which businessmen face. The objective of these discussions is to illustrate ways in which ethical criteria can be brought to bear on problems—and why they have to be applied. *Some* ethic is applied in every situation, for choices imply preferences—even if only to stay *out* of a situation and let another apply his ethical judgments.

To illustrate the penetration of values into many aspects of our lives, let us examine the value of truth or truthfulness. From the standpoint of business, this issue is related to disclosure of information to all of the parties involved—customers through advertising, stockholders through annual reports, workers through internal communications, the public through PR releases, the government through official reporting, and so forth. Conversely, business is concerned to have accurate information from those with whom it deals, including suppliers, customers, government agencies, and workers.

Free enterprise and competition are *founded* on truth. Much business is conducted on the basis of oral and written promises—which implies truth—of future complete compliance. Without it, business could be conducted only with difficulty. Competition requires that "full," or all relevant, information be available to participants in the market. Otherwise, some would make decisions under the "partial duress" of ignorance, giving others an advantage. Of course, since information is not free, there is also a market for information. At the 1979 United Nations Conference on Science and Technology for International Development, one of the greatest needs expressed by developing countries was for access to information on sources of information on technology. The issue of disclosure is highly complex, and requires some careful thought and action.

Before we get into details, however, it is useful to distinguish between searching for truth and speaking the truth. We are concerned with the latter here, but in the dialogue we are carrying out the former. As in all educational activities, the primary objective is to search for the truth. In any dialogue in which the truth is sought, all communication must be as truthful as we can make it. I found long ago in my teaching that it was disastrous to be facetious in class. Every facetious remark would be noted along with all of those I considered to be truthful. The reason was not that the students were stupid or not paying careful attention. It was that they assumed that a professor always spoke the truth (at least as he saw it). They were not, therefore, attentive to detect inaccuracies or contradictions. One uses a different auditory screen when one is listening to a speaker or a program in which deception or lies are expected. Among seekers of the truth, it is expected of all that they speak the truth, at least as they see it.

There are many activities in which people do not expect "the whole truth and nothing but the truth" to be spoken or disclosed. This does not mean that they do not have a *right* to expect it—simply that they have learned that it is unrealistic to expect it. Many surveys have shown that children are learning this lesson at a very early age. A study done at the Harvard Graduate School of Business Administration some years ago reported widespread cynicism among pre-adolescent children. A group of children ages nine to twelve were asked whether advertising commercials told the truth; twenty-four of the thirty-three children replied that the commercials were untruthful because companies "just want to make money." It is a serious condemnation of our system that children do not believe that those who are seeking to make money will be truthful.

THE RIGHT TO KNOW AND
THE DUTY TO DISCLOSE

Businessmen know that information is power, for he who has information is able to make better decisions in a market than he who does not. In some situations, such as card games, obtaining or passing information may be cheating. It is clear that such information provides power—either the ability to win outright or to reduce significantly the chance of loss. In other situations, information can be damaging, as in a golf tournament when a player learns an opponent has just shot three birdies. Information in business is so valuable that many companies go to great lengths—even industrial espionage—to obtain information about what competitors are doing.

We can quickly see that the disclosure of information must be matched by a right to know on the part of the person receiving the information. Who has the right to know? *What* do they have the right to know? *When* do they have the right to know it? These questions imply further ones, such as for what purpose does one have the right to know. Mere desire to know does not constitute a right to know. Nor does the possession of information imply a duty to disclose it.

The functioning of the capitalistic system requires honest communications—in both written and oral form. Any complex market system, and especially one based on the choices of free individuals, requires that communications be appropriate to the choices to be made. This is why truth in advertising is so important. The customer not only has a *need* to know in order to make his choices, but he has a *right* to know, and to know certain things.

If companies advertising their products had always been providing appropriate and relevant information, they would not have to face the constraints now imposed through the Federal Trade Commission.

Numerous penalties have been imposed on companies for not telling the truth, for making claims which were not substantiated, and making unjustifiable comparisons. In one case, the government directed a pharmaceutical company to warn doctors of the serious side effects of a drug it was producing; the company instead sent out a sales letter urging physicians to make certain that their stocks of "this highly valuable specialty" were adequate.

In order to be certain that companies understand the constraints on advertising imposed by being truthful, the Federal Trade Commission has had to describe the characteristics of "truthfulness." (Once again, it is ominous that the government has to tell us the content of ethical decisions.) Truth in advertising is now characterized as "advertising that is without deception, is intelligible, timely, relevant, complete, and appropriate to the audience."

Deception

Deception implies an intent to deceive. It is quite possible for someone to be deceived out of ignorance of the message which is being given, though the message itself is without any intention to deceive. The line between intention to deceive and the intention merely not to disclose adequately is fuzzy; the proliferation of "double speak" words obscures the distinction even more.

"Double speak" is the use of words juxtaposed so as to be virtually unintelligible, even to an intelligent mind. It is exemplified not only by some kinds of advertising but also by professional jargon and governmental "excessiverbage." The National Council of Teachers of English (40,000 members) concluded that such use of the English language is "more to prevent, confuse, and conceal thought" than to express meanings clearly. It set up a committee on "Public Double Speak." The committee has two major aims; (1) to "combat semantic distortion by public officials, candidates for office, political commentators;" and (2) to study dishonest and inhumane use of language and literature by advertisers, to bring offenses to public attention, and to propose classroom techniques for preparing children to cope with commercial propaganda. Notice that commerce and advertising is second only to political deception.

There are obvious connections between the clear use of language and good management. Confucius reportedly said "A good manager is one who uses the language carefully; with clear communication, his orders will be understood clearly and carried out well." Conversely, only misunderstanding is promoted by such statements as Energy Czar William Simon's, made in 1977 when gas was 50¢ per gallon, that "gasoline prices will not be allowed to go to unreasonable or emotional levels." (I understood this statement only in 1979, when I was in Jamaica and the price of gas was raised from $3.50 to $3.75 per gallon!) Imprecise language leads to imprecision and difficulty in decision making. People who are normally good listeners turn off their understanding, even though their ears may be hearing the actual words. The currency of communication is debased when the purpose is to *appear* to tell the truth without in fact doing so.

Understandable Information

The second characteristic of truthful advertising (or any communication) is that it must be intelligible. It must be devoid of "double speak," so that one knows what the words mean. It must also be intelligible to the people to whom it is addressed—the people who are making the decisions to purchase. For example, I recently heard an advertisement for a rally sports car which started off by saying that the information given in the advertisement was not for everybody, but if the listener was interested in the technical capabilities of the auto, here were the facts. The announcer went on to list a series of technical specifications which would make sense only to a car buff. Others would want different kinds of information about their autos. It is not the responsibility of the seller to find out the intelligence quotients of each of the buyers, and to meet his needs precisely, but it is his responsibility to supply information to any customer who seeks it in a way which he can understand. It also is his responsibility *not* to play on the known ignorance of the buyer— as might be in the case in sales of houses, used cars, insurance policies, and so forth. (Of course, many sales people do not know their product well enough to answer simple questions of fact, much less of differences in performance.)

Timeliness

The third characteristic is timeliness. The information should come out in time to be used in making choices in the market.

Relevance

The fourth characteristic is that the information should be relevant. It should not merely be truthful in the sense of accuracy. It should also convey information which is useful in helping individuals make their decisions. Information could be truthful, intelligible, and timely and *still* not be of the sort which would assist people in making certain decisions. For example, the "fact" that *Total* has more vitamins (added) than "a leading natural cereal" may be true, but it's also irrelevant, since one seeks carbohydrates from natural grains and few vitamins; also *numbers* of vitamins says nothing about the quantity of each. Different buyers will have different needs, of course, but information should be available if it is relevant to the buyer's decision, and irrelevant information should not be used to obfuscate.

Completeness

Fifth, the information should be complete. Not that *all* information should be given, for that is simply too much. The absurdity of the demand for "complete information" is shown in the request of a former U.S. Secretary of Commerce, when he was newly appointed to his post, to have a copy of *all* of the publications of the Department delivered to his house so that he could read them over the weekend. He was concerned that too many reports and journals were being published, and he wished personally to cull them. That evening he was astounded to see a small delivery van back up to his garage with two tons of periodicals—and this represented only one month's output by the Department! "Complete" means only "all *relevant*" information desired by the consumer. Essentially, it means that nothing which is useful to the consumer and which he wants to have should be hidden from him.

Appropriateness

Finally, truth in advertising involves appropriate segmentation. What is appropriate—relevant and intelliglble—to adults is not necessarily appropriate for children, for example. And what is often used to persuade children to buy products is itself not appropriate or ethically justifiable.

If companies recognized the necessity to follow the ethical foundations of capitalism in order to maintain a free society, we would not need the government to tell us what is truth in advertising. But profit appears to come before truth in the priorities of some companies.

DUTY TO DISCLOSE

The right to know and the duty to disclose is not restricted to the activity of advertising, however. It extends throughout all business dealings, and includes communications by the government as well. For example, one of the large food chains was charged not long ago with unethical conduct in its negotiations with a milk supplier. It had represented to the bidder that it had a "better offer" from another supplier, and was thus able to drive down the price from this particular bidder. It was later discovered that the food chain did *not* have an alternative offer but was simply using this tactic as a ploy. The supplier sued in court. This was hardly honest communication and it soured the relationships between the supplier and customer.

The problem raised by the duty to disclose has become acute for lawyers and auditors in dealing with information about a company. In one case, the U.S. Court of Appeals in Chicago ruled that, under certain circumstances, auditors can be held liable to the investing public for not knowing what they should have known about a company. The case involved fraud which stockholders argued the auditors should have uncovered. The auditors in turn argued that they would have had to get information from corporate lawyers, who might have to reveal confidential information in order to be sure that the auditors had all relevant information. The controversy raised the issue of whether auditors could give "unqualified opinions" unless the lawyers gave them full information. The lawyers feared loss of their standing in the company if they had to reveal confidential information. Lost in the dialogue is the question of the public's, or stockholders, right to know.

RIGHT TO KNOW

The meaning of "right to know" has been greatly expanded through the SEC's broadening of its disclosure requirements to include information on each corporation's impact on the society, including environmental impacts, energy savings, equal employment practices, political activities overseas, and other factors. In one case, a security offering of a company had to be withdrawn when it was disclosed that its vice president had not filed his income taxes. Issues of managerial behavior are certainly of concern to stockholders; one must ask how much and what kind of data of this sort is relevant to stockholders' decisions.

Though we cannot be precise about every situation, in principle, each person involved with a company should have all material information available to him which has an impact on his decision-making ability. Without this information, one of the parties is under a type of duress. This principle extends to customers, suppliers, stockholders, employees, community officials, and governmental representatives. However, the information which is "material" is different for each of these, and sometimes supplying one gives information to another which may not be appropriate. A company often develops a bias in favor of giving as little information as it can.

One of the reasons that companies attempt to give little information is the frequent irresponsible use of that information by people who may not have a direct right to it—or even by those who do have a right to it. There have been repeated instances in which information given by company officials to the press or to other sources was inappropriately used or even altered to tell an inaccurate or biased story.

On the international scene, there is a controversy at present between the United Nations Centre on Transnational Corporations and various international companies concerning what kinds of information should be made available to the Centre. The Centre is investigating the activities of a number of the companies. The companies insist that those who will interpret the information are already biased in their view of international business and will not use it objectively. They are therefore reluctant to disclose information other than that which is readily available to the public. Such limited information is not satisfactory to the UN Centre, so governments have been asked to force disclosure of the information and then pass it on to the Centre. If this will be done is not clear at the moment, but the issues which we are discussing will be set at the forefront of that dialogue.

We must conclude that the right to know is matched by a responsibility to use the knowledge in a manner which seeks the truth rather than one which seeks to manipulate, to persuade, or to deceive. This is a heavy responsibility, but unless we accept it, we give support to those who wish to limit information disclosure and thus deny the right of the people to know—which is a right that must be exercised if the society is to remain free.

THE RIGHT TO INQUIRE VERSUS THE RIGHT OR DUTY TO WITHHOLD

These same discussions lead to the question of whether there is a right (or duty) to *withhold* information. There undoubtedly is such a right, stemming from the right of privacy, which has as its converse the right of the inquirer to know what he is seeking. The debates over computer banks, personnel evaluations, disclosure of grades, credit ratings, security clearances, and so forth all reflect a concern about the right of privacy and the right to withhold information.

Once again the dividing lines are not easy to draw, for private behavior in one instance may not be relevant to a particular evaluation, while in another it may clearly be relevant. For example, the use of certain drugs by a student to keep awake prior to exams may be of no concern to anyone but himself, while the use of the same drugs by a traffic controller at an airport would be of considerable concern to his supervisors. Similarly, the private sex life of a company official may be of no importance in terms of his job, while that of a minister would be considered serious and relevant information to his parishioners if it passed the boundaries of behavior acceptable to them.

There are other reasons for withholding information, as when the request is out of simple idle curiosity. For example, when a manager returns home and his wife says, "What happened at the office today?", it is highly unlikely that she wishes to hear everything that transpired or even what was interesting to her husband. She is really asking—if she wants her question answered at all—whether anything took place that would be interesting to her. Withholding information in this instance is certainly not unethical, and in fact the husband may know that the question is purely casual (or rhetorical)—a greeting which will soon be followed by an account of his children's misbehavior. Similarly, someone asking, "how did the golf game go?" does not really want a hole-by-hole replay. We can conclude on the basis of these examples that there is a "right to withhold" information which is relative to the situation.

But is there a *duty* to withhold information? In some cases there is, if for no other reason than not to confuse. For example, a child asking, "what is God?" is certainly not ready for a theological dissertation, nor even the complete views of a Presbyterian elder. Much information must be withheld in an argument, and what is given in reply must be appropriate and relevant to the inquirer. A teacher provides building blocks of knowledge in sequence, withholding much information for which the students are not yet ready. We find the same withholding among the Sufi mystics of Arabia, who insist that their students prepare for 40 or 50 years before embarking on the road to enlightenment.

The withholding of information by a government, however, leads to censorship, which, to be warranted, must be fully justified in the public's mind. BBC radio has built a worldwide reputation on its record of not withholding information—even though it might be embarrassing to the British government, which owns the BBC. It is the BBC, not the Voice of America or other broadcasting systems, that is listened to all over the world as the unparalleled source of unbiased reporting. According to a report by Bernard D. Nossiter in the *Washington Post* (January 16, 1977), it obtained this reputation through "a very well established tradition, buttressed by three or four individuals" who would not compromise objectivity and truthfulness. On many occasions, other agencies of the British Government have attempted to edit copy or dissuade the directors from putting out certain news. The most they have succeeded in doing is delaying a story that might be sensitive to *other* countries in diplomatic negotiations, and only then when the story was not directly germane to the news of the day. As a consequence of the station's reputation, BBC reporters are considered "newsmen" by their colleagues in the private media, while Voice of America reporters are considered civil servants. BBC reporters have a wide reputation for "getting it right," and letting complaints fall where they may.

Companies have a limited right to know about the activities of people related to them; they also have a limited right to withhold information from those who inquire about company activities. The exercise of both of the rights is subject to criteria of acceptability formed by the society within which the company operates. These criteria may change. Indeed, they are likely to change—and adversely to the company—if it does not voluntarily operate within the bounds of acceptability. It is because of a presumed lack of relevant and necessary information that the Organization for Economic Cooperation and Development (a sort of rich countries' club) has declared it necessary for companies to "voluntarily" disclose information concerning their international operations—so that governments, the public, and labor can form judgments about the impact of international operations. How companies can be *expected* to provide information *voluntarily* is another issue, but this shows the importance that is attached to information disclosure.

A significant aspect of information disclosure is that the process of disclosing the information itself tends to induce more ethically acceptable behavior on the part of the actors. When I joined the Department of Commerce in 1961 under Secretary Luther Hodges, he gave us one prescription for making certain that our actions were acceptable: "Whatever you do or decide, do so under the supposition that it will appear in the paper the next morning." This stricture *does* alter behavior. A study by MBA students at San Diego State University some years ago showed that the responses of persons interviewed about how they would act in hypothetical situations were altered significantly when they were told in follow-up questioning that they should assume that their responses would be made public.

There is no doubt that our entire lives would be significantly different if we knew that our friends and relatives—to say nothing of the general public—would know about everything we did. (It is interesting to note that we apparently do not believe that God is privy to our thoughts and actions, or, if so, that His view is more important than that of the "general public.")

THE RIGHT TO INVESTIGATE
VERSUS THE DUTY TO DECEIVE
OR THE RIGHT TO LIE

We now turn to the most difficult aspect of truth and disclosure—the right to lie. We can quickly dispense with the question of whether there *is* such a right by arguing the extreme. (These examples are distinctly culture-bound and not directly extendible to all countries of the world.)

There is certainly a right to lie to protect life, just as there is a right of the prisoner of war to withhold information from the enemy concerning troop movements or other activities of his unit. I doubt that anyone would have condemned a mother for lying about the age of her baby in Herod's time, when soldiers came in search of children under two years of age. Nor would anyone condemn a father for lying about the presence of his wife or daughter if they were endangered by an intruder. Two things are noteworthy about these examples, however: they clearly establish a right to lie, but that right is constrained by the *acceptability* to others of the act of lying.

It is carrying the virtue of truthfulness to an extreme to expect anyone to tell an intruder where someone is hiding, when it is obvious that injury will be the result. An exception is the case of a minister in Germany during World War II who asserted that since he could *not* tell a lie, he would, if harboring a Jew in his home, disclose that fact if questioned by SS or other officials. The truthfulness of his assertion was never tested, of course, so we do *not* know if he was telling the truth even then. One may lie to protect one's *own* life if endangered, or conversely, in order to sacrifice one's life in favor of another. Both are understandable and acceptable at times by the community.

Lying should not be confused with "false witness," which is prohibited in one of the Ten Commandments. False witness can occur in a situation in which the judges have a clear "right to know" and in which there is a procedure for determining acceptability of the acts under examination. Bearing false witness, therefore, would be likely to perpetrate or perpetuate an injustice. It would harm someone who should *not* be harmed. One gives witness, furthermore, under oath to tell the truth—an oath given before God or in His name. The protection of "public acceptability" is removed, and only God judges the acceptability of a lie. For secular purposes, a judge takes this part, and perjury becomes itself a crime.

Once we get away from the extremes, it is much more difficult to ascertain the correct applications of the right to lie. The criteria are the same—protection in extremis and acceptability to the public— but it's less easy to determine when and how they should be applied.

It is not acceptable to lie or deceive for the purpose of personal advantage or for the advantage of a superior. Thus, the false testimony of a government official, during hearings on the appointment of Bert Lance as Director of OMB, was considered unacceptable when discovered in later investigations—particularly since the reason the individual lied was because he believed his job would be at stake if he criticized Mr. Lance and was sure that Mr. Lance would be appointed as Director, anyway. Neither is the public inclined to accept deception on the part of a government official dealing with domestic policy issues. This is the reason for the "sunshine laws" passed recently to expose the discussions of government officials with outside consultants or advisors. The Freedom of Information Act is also directed at providing the public with adequate information. The assumption underlying all of these laws is that people will be more honest when they know that what they say is public information. Although there is considerable *acceptable* secrecy with reference to domestic government policy, it is not acceptable to the public that officials deceive Congressmen or lie concerning their policy positions or activities.

When one enters the international realm, the acceptability of deception and lying increases. In this arena, the purpose of deception is not to deceive the domestic populace but to throw off the enemy. Protection of the national security becomes an acceptable justification for lying. Similarly, the protection of a currency against speculative attacks may also be acceptable grounds for lying. No Minister of Finance would admit an intention to devalue the currency, even though he may have already planned and scheduled it. In such cases, the inquirer does not expect that the truth is likely to be told, and is therefore not deceived even though he is lied to.

There is thus a distinction between willful and successful deception on the one hand, and "honest" lying, which does not deceive, on the other. For example, one would expect an FBI or CIA agent to lie in order to protect his cover or that of another agent; it is part of the game that is being played. But when lying or deception is not expected, it is all the more successful. An example of this is the case of a Washington lobbyist who was called before a Congressional committee to explain a letter he had written to his employer concerning contact with a certain Senator. The Senator denied ever having seen the man, though the letter implied that he had been interviewed by and had given information to the lobbyist. The letter stated in part, "In response to your concern about the above issue, Senator ——————— and I had lunch on Wednesday. I can assure you that his position is as follows ——." The lobbyist was asked to explain his reference to a luncheon. He replied, "That is very simple. I never *said* that I met the Senator nor that we had lunch together. I had lunch Wednesday, and I assumed that the Senator had lunch Wednesday. My statement is therefore accurate to the best of my knowledge, and it is certainly not false." All that may be true, but it is certainly a deception, and a willful one.

There are times in which the inquirer *wishes* to be deceived, and is quite happy to be told what he wants to hear, though it is different from the truth. Several editorials concerning Secretary Kissinger's diplomatic style observed that he had a knack for telling people what they wanted to hear, letting different parties proceed on quite different perceptions of the situation simply because he had emphasized those aspects which were pleasing to them. As one columnist put it, "Americans wanted to hear that there were no commitments, so Kissinger told them there were none"—meaning no *written* commitments. General Thieu wanted to hear that there *were* commitments, so Kissinger told everybody there were "moral" commitments, and gave Thieu *oral* commitments. As one columnist saw it, Kissinger was willing to deceive Congress and the public as to exactly what had been done or pledged in their name. Such tactics are likely eventually to catch up with the perpetrator, however, as was the case with a loan agreement with the Egyptians in which Kissinger promised to lend Egypt $80 million before Congress had given its approval. Delays in Congress caused the Egyptians to believe that Kissinger had deceived them and that the U.S. was not keeping its promises.

Whether or not deception was the intent in these cases, it was perceived as such by many observers. Senator Stevenson of Illinois criticized Kissinger's tactics, saying, "A great power does not puruse its interests with bribes, false promises, and gesticulations upon the stage of world opinion." The result was that Congress attempted to limit the Secretary of State's freedom of action and Kissinger bitterly complained. One columnist observed that Congress had been driven to that point "by its feeling that this Secretary of State, more than

any in memory, secretly commits the country to doubtful proposi-
tions. Even when Congress does set guidelines, he is adept at slithering
past them . . . . Resentment at slippery tactics and deception is
catching up with Kissinger."

I'm not concerned here with the merits of what Kissinger was
doing nor with his own personal behavior or the evaluation of his
career. I am concerned about the *perception* of deception on the part
of Congress and the American public, as well as possibly some
foreigners. While it may be acceptable to the American public to
deceive a foreigner, it is not acceptable to deceive our own officials.
Yet secrecy frequently turns out that way. That is, it hides the facts
not only from the enemy but also from those in the U.S. who need
to know. In a newspaper article assessing the effects of secrecy during
the Vietnam War, McGeorge Bundy, former National Security Advisor to Johnson, argued that the perils of secrecy were greater than
the dangers of excessive Presidential power, by hiding the facts from
those who needed to make well-informed decisions. Of course, it is
also debatable whether Congress can be trusted with secret information, or whether telling it to Congress so it can make better plans
isn't also telling the enemy. A wry comment about this circulated in
upper circles of the U.S. Intelligence Community during its pilloring
before Congress: "When is a secret not a secret? When it is disclosed
to a committee of Congress." One highly placed administrative official charged that "The events of the past year have demonstrated
Congress' inability to keep secrets. Kiss-and-tell is not a game to
play when the national security is at stake."

One problem with secrecy is, of course, that it also permits stupidity and errors to be kept covered up rather than disclosed as they
should be in order to correct them. The two sides of this argument
were articulated by Senators Tower and Church during a Congressional debate. Tower: "There comes a point when the people's
right to know must be subordinated to the people's right to be
secure." Church: "In a Democratic society, there should be a strong
preference in favor of letting the people know what their Government is doing. Keeping unlawful programs secret can only serve to
weaken intelligence efforts." They pose the problem, although they
do not answer it.

DIFFERENCES OF DEGREE

There are significant differences between secrecy and deception, between deception and lying, between lying and mere nondisclosure, between not disclosing some information and providing

all relevant information, and between providing relevant information and telling "the whole truth." Telling the whole truth is required in situations such as in court, when the provider of information may not fully understand the relevance of all that he knows. The relevance is determined by someone else—by the judge or the jury. In this instance, information must be disclosed even though its relevance may not be understood by the holder.

The scope of relevant information may sometimes be decided by the government or by the person or company who holds the information: it may not require the whole truth. Nondisclosure of information does not mean that relevant information has been withheld. And, nondisclosure—or "no comment"—is certainly not lying, but it may be deceiving. Lying which is expected is not deceiving; or is lying when in fact the hearer knows better. In the case of the U-2 flight over Russia, President Eisenhower lied about the activity to the Soviet Government but did not deceive them, because they had full information already. Eisenhower's lie was expected and accepted by the public, but it was diplomatically foolish, and he soon told the truth. Secrecy, likewise, is not always deception, although it certainly can be.

In applying ethical criteria to these distinctions, the basic consideration is the acceptability of the act in terms of the *public* interests rather than personal interests. Richard Helms, former Director of CIA, tried it both ways. He was given only small punishment for lying to Congress about certain activities of the CIA; he justified his lie on the grounds that, had he answered truthfully, he would have disclosed other more important operations which were in the national interest to keep secret—though the ones about which he was being questioned were not themselves in the national interest. When he was indicted for perjury, however, he let it be known that if he were to be given serious punishment, he would testify concerning these same secret activities in a way which would damage the national interest. He was unwilling to disclose, ostensibly on the basis of saving the country's skin, but willing to disclose in order to save his own.

The criteria on which to base such difficult judgments must be related to the public interest rather than self–interest. In the final assessment, lying or deception needs to be approved by the relevant public as being in the interest of all others, or as acceptable behavior for any individual in similar circumstances.

In the next chapter, we will look at some of the results of having deceived ourselves about the nature and causes of one of the most pressing problems of today—inflation.

DISCUSSION QUESTIONS

1. What is the origin of the "right to know" of any group in society or society itself *vis a vis* business activities?
2. What types of information does a business have the right to withhold from each of the following?
   a. Stockholders?
   b. Own managers?
   c. Board of Directors?
   d. Workers?
   e. Customers?
   f. Competitors?
   g. Government?
   h. Special interest groups?
3. What will happen if business refuses to disclose information relevant to policy decisions by society?
4. How can companies go about disclosing information appropriately?
   a. Should the process be centralized?
   b. Should procedures be codified?
   c. Should each individual manager decide?

SELECTED READINGS

Bok, Sissela. *Lying: Moral Choice in Public and Private Life.* New York: Pantheon Books, 1978.

Donaldson, Thomas, and Patricia H. Werhane. *Ethical Issues in Business.* Englewood Cliffs, N.J.: Prentice-Hall, 1979, pp. 37–67.

Mintz, Morton, and J. S. Cohen. *Power, Inc.* New York: Viking Press, 1976.

Shonfield, Andrew. *Modern Capitalism.* Fair Lawn, N.J.: Oxford University Press, 1965, Part IV.

Chapter 8

The "Rip-Off" Society: Income Distribution as a Cause of Inflation

Let us now bring some of our earlier thinking to bear on the problem of inflation and see if we cannot discover a basic reason why the problem is so intractable. The reason is found in one of the long unresolved problems of Capitalism and our varied responses to it— that of income distribution.

PRODUCTION AND DISTRIBUTION

The two major economic problems have long been identified as the production of goods and services and the distribution of income. Joseph Schumpeter argued that the second could not be effectively attacked until the first was resolved—that is, socialism could not be afforded until capitalism had raised production to satisfactory levels. The United States and most European countries have now reached income levels that permit them to turn major attention to income distribution, but they have done so only on an *ad hoc* basis. The present inflationary pressure is a direct result of *not* having made income distribution an equal concern of *economic policy*, along with maintenance of production, and of *not* recognizing that the two are inextricably tied together. Income without work (production) affects adversely *both* the receiver and giver; work without equitable income is done inefficiently. When income is taken by governments for welfare distribution, the motivation to produce of the payer and receiver is reduced, and the receiver's "need to be needed" remains unfulfilled when he gets income without performance. Productivity falls when workers consider that take-home pay is inadequate and cannot be raised proportionately with greater effort.

Income distribution relates not only to the flow of wages, rents, profits and so forth, but also to the *composition* of production—that is, goods and services for low-income earners or private vs. public goods and services—and the structure and location of production that is necessary to provide appropriate *opportunities* for employment and income.

Neither economists nor government officials have been willing to give the same attention to developing a system with acceptable income distribution as they have to creating aggregate income, production, and employment. Their assumption is that a larger pie *permits* all to have more, and thus all will be satisfied. But the size of the pie says *nothing* of the size of the slices, who gets them, what kind of pie it is, who had the pleasure of making it, nor whether the satisfaction of people in work and acceptability of income affects the size and quality of the pie itself.

Until we integrate the process of production and distribution, we will continue to sustain inflation—at least given our present system. If we cannot resolve inflation, we will also be prevented from solving the problem of unemployment. Unemployment exacerbates the injustices of the income distribution system, and inflation makes the inequities both more evident and less bearable. Consequently, the system is perpetually disturbed, making it ripe for radical change—change which, according to the French journalist Jean-François Revel, will occur in the U.S. "Without Marx or Jesus." It is only by grasping firmly the problem of income distribution that we will be able to achieve a just and equitable economic system and thereby relieve one of the primary causes of continued inflation.

INCOME REDISTRIBUTION

The causes of inflation have been approached from many angles, with conflicting proposals for its remedy. Confusion reigns in the minds of analysts largely because of their unwillingness to see that inflationary pressures arise from *dissatisfaction* with the distribution of income and the increasing ability of various groups to alter the distribution through economic and political *power*. These two concepts are key: dissatisfaction, which means that criteria of equity either do not exist or are not met; and power to change distribution, outside or inside the market.

Redistribution occurs through the raising of prices and wages *or* taxes. The power to tax is the power to *transfer* income; the power to raise prices above competitive levels is similar to the power to tax; and the power to raise wages above productivity levels is also the power to take from others.

Couple the drive for material gain with the ability of several groups to *acquire* income—not through production but through altering its distribution—and the result will be an increasing pressure on prices. This pressure could be restrained by strong ceilings on the money supply, but only with unacceptable levels of unemployment and further distortions in production patterns and relative incomes. Both would lead to wage and price controls—and socialism, according to Schumpeter and Friedman. Yet this is the prescription of many economists—or the dilemma which prevents their prescribing at all.

A perceptive article on the problem by two economists noted that—

> Conventional economics is in confusion, or worse, crisis. Unable to offer any cure for inflation but unemployment, it proposes to cure smallpox with typhus, cancer with plague . . . Wassilly Leontief has summed it all up: "One reason why economists are in such disrepute is that they have pretended to understand inflation and to know how to control it when obviously we do not." Or, listen to Paul Samuelson: "No jury of expert economists can agree on a satisfactory solution or diagnosis for the modern disease of stagflation" (*Forbes*, November 15, 1976).

RESPONSE TO TAXES

One of the reasons for the inadequacy of economic analysis is lack of recognition of the importance of tax policy, as distinct from fiscal policy, in the institutional setting of modern capitalism as we described it previously. Fiscal policy relates to the relative income and outgo of governments; *tax* policy with the composition and level of taxes; and expenditures policy with the level and composition of government spending. Government expenditures inject more money into the system, but they would *not* be inflationary *if* taxes took equal spending power from the public and private sectors—and, of course, if government spending could be applied to more inflation-sensitive sectors of the economy, such as military material, than would have been the case if funds had not been taxed, especially since the latter are composed of income that would have otherwise gone into savings. The private sector will attempt to off-set (regain) the taxes when it has the power to do so. As the government official responsible for wage and price guidelines, C. Jackson Grayson, Jr. observed, "Neither business nor labor is very satisifed with any given distribution of their share of income at any given time. Both will seek to improve their share." (*Challenge*, November/December, 1974). And both have that power in our present structure because of the removal of constraints on competition and steward-ship in private property, as well as the rise of unions and special interest groups. The exercise of this power will raise prices (and wages) to offset the loss of taxes, passing them on to the consumer. Leonard Silk, is a column for *The New York Times*, stated succinctly that "Inflation is a consequence of the way massive organizational pressure-group economies operate"—creating a continuous spiral of inflation. Instead of focusing on the underlying reasons why these groups act to cause inflation and what might be done to satisfy their basic concerns, Silk concluded that "An effective program against inflation must be one that faces up to the necessity of curbing the power of the special interests and removing their corrupting influence on government."

Rather, we should face up to the fact that special interest groups will form in a democracy whenever the existing distribution of benefits is unacceptable or when they can be reallocated in their favor. The only long-run solution is to develop an acceptable system of distribution—not suppress the political process of redress by special interest groups. Such groups are not always "corrupting"; in fact, they may help redress the existing system when it is inequitable. Their pressure will subside or be counterbalanced effectively only if the system is seen as equitable and acceptable.

The government is increasingly taxing for the *purpose* of rectifying an unacceptable distribution of income in the society—through increases in the minimum wage, in social security, in unemployment benefits, in welfare payments, aid to education, medicare and medi-caid, housing subsidies, urban redevelopment, and so forth. All of these measures raise taxes, which are passed on in price increases, and shift income from savings to spending, altering the patterns of consumption and production. Women are moving increasingly into the labor force to regain lost (real) income, thereby raising demand and increasing price pressures, which tend to depress wages, which in turn is fought by demands for higher wages and unemployment benefits. The latter are doubly inflationary since more money chases fewer goods.

We are faced, then, with unacceptable inflation and unacceptable unemployment because we have failed to face up to the fact that a root cause lies in an unacceptable distribution of income and the pattern of opportunities. The concern for reduction of inflation *and* greater equity in incomes would not automatically disappear with wage and price controls (or guidelines, as proposed, "where necessary"). Rather, controls increase the visibility of inequities in the system. The results of control must be seen as *clearly* equitable if they are to gain acceptability. This leads immediately to the questions of "fair prices" and the "just wage." These, in turn, raise the problem of comformance to generally accepted standards of equity, which themselves are likely to shift according to the movement of the populace to the right or left.

PROPOSALS

In a special issue on inflation, the editors of *Business Week* (September 14, 1974) stated that

> Economists are beginning to recognize this process as a pyramiding of competing income claims. The various sectors of the economy—labor and management, for instance—are constantly pushing for a larger share of total income. Their demands keep adding up to more than 100% of gross national product no matter how fast it grows.

But this assertion is not followed by any suggestion that what is fundamentally at issue is the unwillingness to accept market–determined incomes—to apply different concepts of equity (or *no* concepts, in an effort simply to *get* more). This unwillingness affects productivity and therefore impacts both "demand management" policies *and* supply generation. Inflation, of course, accentuates this unwillingness because of its uneven impacts on different segments of the economy.

Rather than recognizing the dual impacts on government policies and supply of production, and proposing remedies, *Business Week* proposed the following:

"The only real answer to the problem of competing income claims is to keep total output rising"—as though an ever-increasing pie would settle who got the larger pieces!

"A maze of government regulations and special interest legislation obstructs the efficient working of the market place"—as though various income-groups were interested in efficiency and would accept dismantling of their hard-won protective programs!

"All industrial countries will have to begin thinking of more efficient use, recycling, and development of less extravagant life styles"— as though this could be done without asking the fundamental question of how this can be done through the market place or what *right* any group has to any given standard of living, both within and among nations—that is, the questions of equity and sharing.

"They must also find a way to make the oil-producing countries realize that the present prices on crude are intolerable"—as though there were some readily or generally known or accepted criteria of "tolerable" ("fair" or "equitable"?) prices. (Are those criteria market-determined or are they derived from philosophical, ethical, metaphysical, or theological concepts?)

Each of these suggestions avoids the issue of the *criteria* of equity and the relation of income distribution to the *process* of production and the types of job opportunities—*despite* the fact that each proposal involves a redistribution of incomes. Most suggestions in the popular press aim at sustaining high income levels within privileged groups, including the U.S. as a whole *vis à vis* other nations. Such a skewed distribution might be justified by *some* criteria, but it is unlikely that any power group will accept market-dictated criteria unless they operate in its favor. The U.S. certainly won't, when faced with an oil monopoly, though monopolies operate through a market! We are not trying seriously to come up with anything to substitute for market criteria of fairness. As a consequence, the power of quasi-monopolistic and monopolistic groupings of business, labor, and *any* other income recipients will continue to be employed through the market *and* outside of it.

EQUITY: THE ISSUE

In article after article on inflation, the problem of equity is raised and pushed aside, not to be included in the major points of discussion. Yet a more eclectic analysis of the situation leads to the conclusion that equity in income distribution is one of the root causes of the present inflation, and will remain so until the problem is grasped firmly.

As the two journalists mentioned earlier concluded from their examination of inflation over 1,000 years, "Inflation is not—as

Maynard Keynes thought and Milton Friedman thinks—a simple matter with social consequences. It is an infinitely complicated business with social causes" (*Forbes*, November 15, 1976).

Without addressing the problem of social objectives of price and tax increases, all of the technical nostrums relating to monetary and fiscal policies will merely obfuscate the issues, and we will continue to risk high unemployment and the waste of resources through "stop, go" policies.

It is readily understandable why economists have avoided the problem. To recognize income distribution as a major *cause* of inflation is "unacceptable" to many economists, for it strikes at the very basis of their concept of the "proper working" of the economy. Income distribution is supposed to be a *result*, not a cause, of a free and "properly functioning" market. Most economists refuse to recognize that every group with any economic or political *power* will be unwilling to accept the income–distributing results of the market as long as there are no socially acceptable (or enforceable) criteria of income determination.

INCOME FROM CONTRIBUTION

John Stuart Mill observed in the mid-nineteenth century in his *Principles of Economics* that there were "laws of production of goods" but no "laws of distribution of income." One of the stabilizing factors in Western economies has been that the populace has generally accepted the view that income *should be* received according to the distinct contribution of each producer, despite the fact that such contributions have never been calculable. Contribution was to be determined in a market, according to Adam Smith, guided by an "invisible hand." The concept of income according to contribution is supposed to prevent one from reaping where he does now sow. That is, economic or political power is not *supposed* to be used to vary or distort the distribution of income. Each individual is supposed to have an opportunity to contribute according to his talents.

Increasing moves by business, labor, and government away from a self–regulating market and towards oligopolistic structures in major markets have resulted from efforts by each of the players in the economic system to gain additional income through power rather than through contributions of greater value. One result is the wage-price push. Neither business nor labor is willing to leave its power, economic or political, unexercised; both use it to acquire more material wealth to maintain what they have in the face of rising taxes. Each does so in the belief that "he is successful who has the greater material means." Merely "making a living" is not a sufficient criterion. Rather, to be successful, we must have more and more—both absolutely and relatively. (Happiness, of course, could be gained by merely "making a living," rather than amassing material wealth. But in a system where distribution is a *result* of production, the primary goal has to be material progress for society as a whole. The criteria became material and measurable. It comes down to money, rather than psychic income.)

CONTINUED PRESSURES

Inflation feeds on itself, both quantitatively and socially. It accelerates the drive for increased *relative* income shares, for it makes each group feel that it is being or may be left behind through the *redistribution* of income that results from inflation. It is generally recognized that certain groups—people with fixed incomes, pensioners, and unemployed—are seriously damaged by inflation. What is becoming increasingly clear is that nearly *all* groups are damaged by inflation at some time or another, particularly since the tax burden rises under progressive income schedules. Even corporations are damaged through falling real profits, despite rising money profits. Each can mitigate this damage only by exercising economic power. The classic reaction to increase production in times of inflation is impeded by shortages and rapidly rising costs. It is then seen as better to produce less and to try to raise prices faster, as was the case with metals prices in late 1975.

Those who cannot raise prices turn to political activity in order to maintain their income share. This has been done successfully by farm groups, federal pensioners, utilities, welfare-recipients, corporations, state government employees, unemployed, and many others.

When the checks and balances of the capitalist system—that is, a self-regulating, competitive market, stimulated by economic motivation relying on a socially sensitive use of *private* (not corporate) productive property, and operating under rules enforced by the government—when those checks and balances no longer exist, all that remains is the motivation of material gain, exercised by whatever means are available. The result: greed + power = inflation; or, a rip-off society!

From the first, when sovereigns caused inflation by clipping or debasing the coinage, one group or another in society has been damaged. A group will seek to protect itself or add to its material gains through redistributing the benefits in its favor. Without acceptable criteria of equity in income distribution, and the checks of the market—itself now seen as producing an unacceptable distribution—we will face continuing inflation, for which we will be provided technical analyses and conflicting solutions, each attempting to find an answer to the wrong questions. The social *consequences* can be devastating, for a general view of the system as unfair leads to critical breakdowns—as with the looting in New York in the blackout last year, the vandalism and stealing in St. Croix, or a willingness to "rip off" a hotel or company because the "system is unfair" or "prices are excessive anyway." A society *does* live by its value system—whatever it may be—though its not necessarily the one it asserts. A search for justice in an unbalanced economic system can bring down the entire social system.

The evidence abounds that an unacceptable income distribution is a key cause of inflation. Yet economists are unwilling to place it high among their analytical priorities. The economists invited in the fall of 1974 to advise President Ford were urged by one of their members *not* to get bogged down in assessing the problem of income distribution, and that advice has been firmly followed both before and since.

THE PRIORITY PROBLEM

The problem of income distribution *should* have high priority, for it is a primary reason for the decline of free market decisions. Competitive industries such as lumber and wood products, farm products, hides and leather, and processed foods have sought—and gained, on occasion—protection through governmental legislation. Others that *were* competitive, such as airlines, textiles, mushrooms, iron and steel, have sought private agreements or governmentally sponsored ones extending to tariffs, quotas, and "orderly marketing agreements" in the international arena. The more concentrated industries, and many under governmental regulation—iron and steel, autos, utilities, petroleum, rubber, machinery, and tobacco—have been able to raise and maintain high prices in the face of declines in demand and increased taxes. The extent of private and governmental interference in the market reflects an unwillingness of those with power, whether economic or political, to accept the results of a free market. Many who have refused had good reason: there is nothing in a market mechanism *per se* to guarantee equity in income distribution. Equity results from *other* aspects of the economic system than the market itself; the market merely clears supply and demand—regardless of how the income was earned or whether it was justly deserved.

REJECTION OF MARKET CRITERIA

Interference in the market by state government also reflects an unwillingness of producers and sellers to accept market results. Examples are prohibitions on advertising the prices of eyeglasses or drugs, which prevent customers in some states from knowing competitive prices among sellers; "fair trade" laws which rigidify the workings of the market; floors under milk prices and regulated rates on insurance policies; occupational licensing that is used to restrict entry; protection of "professional groups" through entry procedures; and mandating of state purchases from in-state businesses rather than less costly, out-of-state sources.

Private efforts are not restricted to altering the operations of the market: they include clearly illegal acts. Scarce supplies have permitted some companies to allocate orders at "established" prices to customers and then to charge prices several times higher to fill orders above allocations—sometimes through "back door" arrangements. Consumers have fought back with their own techniques—returning used merchandise for full credit, switching price labels, pilfering and shoplifting, inflating claims for damaged goods and lost merchandise, and making fraudulent insurance claims—none ethically acceptable.

The breakdown of honesty extends through the system and leads to a situation like that of countries where tax honesty is a joke and the basic orientation is to beat the system rather than to support it. Such an orientation occurs when the system is no longer acceptable—when it is seen as not worth saving—and a new paradigm or model is sought. Irresolution and mini-chaos result when there is no clear model of behavior to substitute for the existing one, despite its inapplicability or unacceptability. This is our situation in 1980.

MAJOR PROPOSALS

Current proposals to cure inflation contain two major policy directions: a return to "free market" determinations by closer regulation of monopolistic elements, breaking up concentrations in industry, and removal of governmental interferences; or alternatively, an increase in government control and guidance to the private sector, capped by nationalization of key industries. Neither is acceptable or workable without an accompanying criterion for "acceptable distribution" of the benefits. Neither proposal solves the problem automatically; both require the application of criteria of equity.

Some proposals seem to recognize this fact but fail to come to grips with it in the precise mechanisms offered. For example, G. William Miller, before his appointment as Chairman of the Federal Reserve Board and later, Treasury Secretary, stated that "The problem of arresting inflation is today more political and social than economic. The task is to find an economic solution that is politically acceptable because it accommodates society's value goals" (*Business Week*, October 5, 1975). He did not say what these value goals are, and his solutions do not meet the problem of income distribution. He would restrain consumption, without saying *who* is to consume less. He would encourage personal savings and investment, without saying who is to have the income to save. He would spur business investment and productivity and declare a moratorium on strikes, without saying how labor is to get a fair income for its increased productivity. And he would inaugurate some emergency and relief programs for businesses and workers, without having first established any criteria of equity for extending such assistance. He concludes that a "program of selective, flexible, and comprehensive actions, relying mainly on allocation by inducement while avoiding undue hardship" is the only approach that "can regain public confidence and provide the best chance of success while preserving our democratic, private enterprise system."

This effort to couple democracy and private enterprise in one system has given us the results we have today because both require an exercise of individual responsibility that we have not achieved. Political democracy eventually provides many groups, though not all individuals, with power—power which is used to redistribute the economic benefits, not necessarily to increase the total pie. Private corporate enterprise is not democratic; its influence on the economy has been to reduce individual competition in favor of large corporate bodies within which individuals function as managers or workers. These individuals soon discover that power within the corporation is gained by political means, as well as by performance, and that power leads to perquisites and wealth. Various national administrations have demonstrated that similar motivations exist among some government officials. Private enterprises have not been averse to using power to realign their positions in the market and to reduce uncertainties. The trend, therefore, has been toward a managed economy, and the greater the management the more everyone sees that the distribution of income is also managed. In this situation, it behooves each to try to use his role to increase his income, which is thus not necessarily a direct result of productivity in market terms.

Otto Eckstein, a former member of the Council of Economic Advisers, was reported (*New York Times*, December 28, 1974) as saying that if we cannot solve the problems of inflation and unemployment, we may have to "change the system" by putting governmental officials on corporate boards or nationalizing critical industries. These are solutions for symptoms and not causes! What is to assure that nationalization will do more than suppress the dissatisfaction rather than assuage it? It has not done so in Britain. Britain's trauma is an excellent example of the costs of not pushing the problem of income distribution to the fore, when the system was disintegrating because of the unacceptable distribution of benefits and perquisites and the increased power of the less advantaged to disrupt the economic order.

EXTENT OF THE PROBLEM AND ITS RECOGNITION

The inequitable condition of the U.S. economy is replicated at the international level. Continuing world tensions and disorder result from the inability and unwillingness of national governments to focus on the problems of social equity and economic justice. One of the reasons for their reluctance is that the West's current paradigm relies heavily on a warped concept of individualism—individual *rights* unmatched by responsibilities, which has been warped even more by the concept of *entitlements*. It consequently denies the desirability of a sense of community, including a concern for social justice and economic equity.

Many people understand this far better than their leaders. A survey by the *Washington Post* surfaced these views from around the country:

A dairy farmer in Wisconsin—

What's the matter with this country is everybody's out for the buck. It's all money. Big money. All they want to do is keep the Mississippi River open. Get the coal there. Get the grain there. I think the only way we're going to stop inflation is for people to consume less. And I can't see any way to do this without a depression.

A Missourian—

I sense in the lives of the people a real hunger for an authentic community that's not involved in making corporate or church decisions, but the kind of community where you can share your hurts and insights. I think we're in the process of acquiring some humility [through a church discussion group]. I think there's a kind of suspicion or weariness or onguardedness about whether or not the institutions and structure of our society are adequate to make the kinds of decisions that have to be made. I have a feeling that for some folks, getting positions of responsibility, fulfilling a function or a role, doing a good job have turned out to be not enough.

Similar perceptions have come from a British financier, Sir Siegmund Warburg:

The speed of the expansion has been overwhelming, and that is the real reason for the inflation from which we are all suffering. And the real reason for the excessive speed of expansion is that governments and peoples have been too impatient—too impatient and too greedy. It may be that this crisis has come to punish our Western World for excessive greed and materialism [interview in *Business Week*, November 13, 1974].

He sees a different world coming out of this punishment, with different forms of government, not necessarily totalitarian in the sense of suppression of freedom.

What may happen as a result of this crisis is that perhaps we will come to a period of less materialism, instead of still higher incomes and still more motor cars, we may have a slightly simpler life with less comfort and more happiness in our Western World. I know it sounds strange coming from a banker, but perhaps it might not be so bad from a human point of view.

Economists have avoided these problems because they require substantial changes in the *institutional structure* of the economy, an aspect which they have decided years ago not to include within their discipline. Institutions are not readily incorporated in market theory, and they do not fit neatly into models which void the problem of power. Inclusion of the concept of power leads to indeterminacy in the theory of gains (*vide*, the theory of games and strategy). Considerations of equity involve value goals, and economics is supposed to be a "value-free" discipline—making it "valueless" in treating the fundamental problem of social welfare and economic development.

For these reasons economists have ignored Gardiner Means' analysis of administered pricing. In a recent article on inflation in the *Democratic Review*, Senator Proxmire emphasized the political nature of the problem and stressed the need to add microeconomic controls over administered prices. He does raise the problem of a "fair return" to industries so controlled, but he does not generalize this question into "fair prices," "fair wages," and "fair incomes." It is interesting to note how quickly the concept of "fair prices" is injected into the debate on the oil problem, that of "fair wages" into the debate on export of U.S. jobs, and that of "fair incomes" in debates on agricultural policies.

It is difficult, policy-wise, to integrate oligopolistic and administered pricing practices or theories. And not enough effort has been made to examine the effects of such practices on an equitable distribution of income. This analysis, along with that of "fair prices," has been left out of the picture. To continue to do so means pursuit of solutions which are as dangerous as bright lights in a heavy fog. One must not only dim the lights; in the long run, the fog must be dispelled. This economic fog can be dispelled only by focusing our energies on the central issue—the acceptability of economic shares in the society, or in other words, economic justice.

It would also help to demote the concern for material advance to *second* place among our economic priorities. Economic goals should be seen not in terms of the piling up of material goods and services, but in meeting specific objectives in the least costly manner. These objectives could be met not with the production of *less* goods, but the production of *different* goods. For example, the transportation needs of the economy might well be achieved by use of *less* resources than at present. Health needs of the society can also be achieved with considerably less goods (food and drugs), especially if more attention were paid to nutrition and health maintenance than to curing of ills. (It is curious that medical services are included in the GNP; if more people were sick more frequently the economy would be seen to be better off, when in fact medical services involve a redistribution of income—and production, since worker (or manager) output falls during illness and medical income rises.)

It is quite conceivable that we could all eat less, be healthier, use less steel in automobiles, dress more warmly and use less energy in heat and, consequently, be *better off* materially with a *lower* GNP, leaving more time for community living, or contemplation—and be happier! Such a reorientation of our thinking towards *least* use of materials to meet specific demands, needs, or pleasures would be likely to release substantial resources for meeting the needs of those not presently served acceptably by the pattern of income distribution.

It would be feasible to spread the income even more equitably through a sharing of the work, with fewer hours for each per week, though not at the same weekly earnings. This would still permit a comparable standard of living, but through the consumption of less wasteful goods and services. Such work sharing is now reported among working wives who want part-time work; companies are accommodating in order to bring these women into the work force.

MINIMIZATION VERSUS MAXIMIZATION

We should reorient our thinking away from *maximizing* gross national *product* and toward *minimizing* gross national *input*, while at the same time increasing the material standard of living and the quality of life *for all*. Such a reorientation would emphasize the interdependence of all factors and groups within the system and would begin to make material advance a secondary goal. This shift would also *substitute* redistribution of work for redistribution of income. Imagine the effects of a shift in attitude away from "making a profit" to "making a living." To "make a living" implies that one is satisfied with a particular (relative?) standard of living within one's community; the objective would be to minimize costs. To "make a profit" has been characterized historically by "maximization" of profit without regard for social consequences, *or* with regard for them only *after* profits were made, rather than during the process itself. Where prices are administered or profits are gained in oligopolistic markets, it *appears* that managers are able to allocate income to themselves. One businessman has stated that "the open scandal of business is the high salaries of top corporate officials," as evidenced by the munificent rewards given to Penn Central managers despite their failure to keep the railway out of bankruptcy.

"RIP-OFFS"

It appears these days that the profit maker reaps where he does not sow. Recent excessive profits have intensified the feeling that business is "ripping-off" the society. Businessmen themselves question the high profits made on occasion in the sugar and petroleum industries. On the other hand, they can and do repeat stories of customers who are trying to "rip-off" sellers, of sellers who are trying to "rip-off" suppliers, and of customers and suppliers who are trying to "rip-off" their business clients through hoarding of materials and fabricated shortages. The proliferation of stories of price gouging, tax evasion, political shenanigans of companies and interest groups, bribery in contracting and procurement, and the blatant use of power by labor unions or groups—the truckers' fights among themselves, for example—give further credence to the view that we are in the midst of a "rip-off" society.

Inflation feeds this view. It broadens the extent of dishonesty in the system, as exemplified by the welching on contracts by suppliers who claim they cannot afford to sell at the prices they had agreed to earlier. The perception of tax dishonesty is increasing, and this perceived destruction of the basic tax honesty of Americans merely intensifies "rip-off" attitudes. Inflation, therefore, tears at the very fabric of social order. It is particularly critical in a time of recession, for it not only voids the use of reflationary policies but accentuates dissatisfaction with the distribution of economic benefits created by the recession.

CONTROLS VERSUS EQUITY

Such deterioration has been stopped in the past only by repressive governments. Dictatorial governments have been called in to establish *order*—an order which is acceptable, if not equitable, because of a stronger desire for stability and survival than for freedom. (J.-F. Revel's *The Totalitarian Temptation* shows that economic crises move countries strongly and "willingly" towards totalitarianism.)

We can reestablish order without repression only by maintaining an *honest* approach to cost, wages, and prices and by achieving an equitable distribution of income. Only then will the *system* again be acceptable. When this is achieved, we can rely less on tax policy to redistribute income; monetary and fiscal policies can be used more easily to regulate the flow of money in relation to goods. Until then, efforts to achieve price stability through aggregate monetary and fiscal policies will fail. Wage and price controls will also fail unless they are seen as equitable by those affected. Unfortunately, those under controls are only a part of the total system, and they will see inequity in the fact that not everyone is under a similar control system. Some will advance under a control system and some will advance outside of it. Those remaining behind will become disaffected and seek to break the system.

NEW ATTITUDES REQUIRED

What is required is a reconstruction of the system based on honesty and stewardship, which will develop an equitable income distribution, and in turn stimulate production of a new sort to raise incomes. Income distribution can no longer merely "fall out" of the production system; the latter must be *directed* to achieve equity in distribution. *Only then* will monetary and fiscal policies be effective; wage and price controls would probably not be needed. This issue has not yet been raised at the necessary policy levels, probably because it means system-wide reconstruction of personal attitudes and motivations—changes, in other words, at the very foundation of capitalism. If it could be recognized that an inequitable distribution of income is a major *cause* of inflation, through public and private efforts to alter that distribution, we might successfully reorder our priorities!

Of course no single-factor analysis can hold up among the complex relationships existing in our politico economic system. We can't lay our problems on income distribution alone. One could also ask why the concern over income distribution, which has always been endemic in the system, is just now accelerating inflation. The answer lies in two additional factors: (1) the increasing assumption by government of responsibility for the acceleration of the drive for economic development, which both pushes demand faster than goods can be supplied and places more economic and social welfare decisions into the *political* arena—increasing redistribution through taxation; and (2) the recent (artificial or real) shortages of basic materials which permit an intensification of scarcity and consequent price increases by manipulation of supplies at the margins. Both factors indicate that our demands are out distancing our performance—a desire, that is, to consume without producing.

The consequences of alternative solutions to the problem of income distribution are not readily discernible at present. Much thought needs to be given to the results of changing patterns of income production and distribution under alternative institutional structures. Such an analysis would lead to consideration of social philosophy and ethical values—subjects largely rejected by economists but inextricably woven into the fabric of political economy. The various aspects that would require analysis include the value goals of society, the impact of different income-distributing mechanisms on motivation, the means of building income distribution into employment programs rather than through redistribution of money income alone, the effects of new patterns of job security on innovation and flexibility in the system, and the changes wrought by reduced growth rates in the economy. If growth rates *must* be reduced, the concern over income distribution will be intensified among the different countries as well as within them.

All this requires careful analysis of a sort for which economists are not currently trained. They will have to take guidance from the "underworld" of economics—from J. S. Mill, Thorstein Veblen, John R. Commons, R. H. Tawney, J. A. Hobson, and even Frank H. Knight, who questioned whether income should be distributed according to contribution when talents were so unequally distributed among potential contributors. Much more attention should also be given to the social philosophies and value systems underlying economic structure. The idea is to match the mechanism to the objectives and to avoid unwanted side-effects, as emphasized by Norbert Weiner in his lectures on the relation of religion to cybernetics. (*God and Golem*, 1970).

The concerns of the early social philosophers over income distribution and institutional structures have been disregarded by 20th century political economists. Because of their failure to look carefully into these problems, their forecasts and nostrums have become increasingly irrelevant and even erroneous—as emphasized in Robert Gordon's 1974 Presidential Address to the American Economic Association. But economists are set in their ways, as shown in the statement by Otto Eckstein (*Business Week*, June 29, 1974): "I'm not going to wait for some political economist to solve the relationship between power, class structure, and the economy before I turn my model loose to get GNP forecasts." Such an assertion demonstrates blind faith in the parameters of a model that has little relationship to the power structures; yet it is just these power structures that limit the relevance of forecasts. Since the market will buy such forecasts, they will be produced, and much capable brainpower will remain diverted from the more fundamental problems.

Economists have abdicated their responsibilities. Others must take the initiative, and they should be among the present leaders of business and government. It is to be hoped that they will give serious consideration to the problem *before* precipitate action is taken to change an unacceptable system. The challenge is none other than the application to the economy of the early underlying ethic so that work and income are commensurate (just) and welfare (public goods) can be restricted to providing equity at the margin, rather than itself altering the motivations in the system. The market will function appropriately to these ends *only* if the system within which it operates provides opportunities for all and rewards honesty, integrity, and playing by acceptable rules. Otherwise, we will have continued interference *in* and *outside* the market, which may produce greater inequity *or* force inflation in an attempt to achieve a more equitable income distribution. The end of such a process is, of course, the removal of freedom—both economic and political.

DISCUSSION QUESTIONS

1. Why have economists, managers, and government officials avoided confronting the problem of income distribution?
2. How is income distribution tied to individual motivation, productivity, and economic growth?
3. What is the relation between inflation (and expectations of continued inflation) and the acceptability of income distribution? How will the following different groups react?
   a. retired persons
   b. workers
   c. managers
   d. stockholders
   e. civil servants
   f. teachers
   g. farmers
4. What should be the basis of income distribution?
   a. How can we institute it?
   b. What business positions will have to be changed?
5. How intensive and extensive will inflation have to become to destroy our present system of freedoms?
   a. Like Germany of the 1920s and 1930s?
   b. Like Brazil of the 1960s and 1970s?

SELECTED READINGS

Behrman, J. N. *Towards a New International Economic Order.* Paris: Atlantic Institute, 1974.
Knight, F. H. *Risk, Uncertainty, & Profit.* New York: Houghton Mifflin Co., 1921, Chap. XII.
Lekachman, Robert. *Economists at Bay.* New York: McGraw-Hill, 1976.
Mintz, M., and J. S. Cohen. *Power, Inc.* New York: Viking Press, 1976.
Revel, J. -F. *Without Marx or Jesus.* Garden City, N.Y.: Doubleday, 1974.
——. *The Totalitarian Temptation*, Garden City, N.Y.: Doubleday, 1977.
Silk, Leonard, and David Vogel. *Ethics and Profits.* New York: Simon & Schuster, 1976.
Wanniski, J. *The Way the World Works.* New York: Simon & Schuster, 1978.

Chapter 9

Codes of Conduct

From many quarters have come proposals that companies and associations, as well as government entities, should prepare and distribute codes of conduct for their members. These proposals have come from board chairmen, from church, civic, union, and university leaders who have considered the responsibilities of organizations to the larger society. A number of companies have such codes, and many have had them for several decades; similarly, a number of trade associations, professional associations, and unions have codes. But the codes are frequently left unenforced when violations occur. There are strong advantages to having codes, especially as the society begins to examine more closely the conduct of various organizations and the individual members—including the Federal Government and Congress.

To many people, the promulgation of a code seems a trivial approach to problems of personal conduct. They expect people to be responsible for themselves: therefore, codes need not and should not exist. However, it is just this lack of personal responsibility, for oneself and one's relationship to others, that is leading to the increased pressure for the development of codes of conduct.

In previous discussions we have touched on a number of changes in society and conditions in the business community which make it necessary to establish ethical codes of conduct for organizations. Among them is the continued willingness to deceive or lie, reinforced by deception in advertising and the "big lie" in politics, both of which undercut honesty in communication. Cheating is winked at in educational institutions, and winning becomes more important than playing by the rules—especially when being on a winning team in college opens the door to professional athletics. Players as well as spectators and university officials are caught in a spiral of degraded ethics. Entire student bodies are caught up in the "anything to win" syndrome—throwing ice on basketball floors and flashing lights in the eyes of a player shooting a foul shot. These individuals enter business with less than extensive exercise in decency. More and more people try to "rip-off" the system, which in turn leads to substantial white collar crime and unethical behavior within the organizations of business and government. Such a trend is costly in terms of economic efficiency as well as personal development.

Ethical training is all but absent in school programs, in churches and YMCA-type groups, and finally in the home. Entire families and particularly children spend much of their time in front of the TV, where dubious conduct is condoned and frequently "successful," and the pursuit of elevating ideas or skills is virtually nonexistent. Only inculcation of concepts of social cohesiveness and responsibility in the exercise of individual creativity can reinforce ethical conduct. This task is the responsibility of the family and the supportive institutions of school and church.

The prevalence of "group-think" in all stages of life and at all levels of social activity also allows ethical conduct to sink below desirable norms. For example, one company executive explained that no single individual officer of his company would have supported a certain unethical decision, but all did when put to them collectively. Further, the decline in confidence in business, social, and political leaders as a result of exposés of illegal and unethical conduct (to say nothing of their pursuit of personal interest above those of the group, and evidences of plain stupidity) further undermines the young individual's reverence for authority or ethical leadership. This in turn leads to scepticism about the motives of superiors; the young business man or woman feels free to select role models from any group, as they see fit. The almost random selection of leadership is reinforced by the lack of a community in which certain groups are clearly seen as the communal leaders and set the pattern of ethical conduct. The absence of community is itself partly a result of increasing mobility within the society, both geographically and in terms of career, which in turn decreases loyalty within the group and eliminates a feeling of "proper place"—leading to the alienation of the individual from social norms. These are replaced by group norms which are frequently contrary to those needed to retain a wider social cohesion.

Finally, the power achieved by the cohesion of smaller, special interest groups leads to the exercise of authority without an adequate counterbalancing responsibility to the larger society. A reconsideration is necessary of the relationship of individual members to their groups and to the society in general. This can be done through the formation, promulgation, and implementation of codes of conduct. Were the same objectives met otherwise, such codes would not be proposed today; these proposals result from the absence of adequate handling of a significant problem.

The problem is illustrated in the report of Harvard Business School students that they are left with the belief that "marketing is amoral," and that there are no marketing ethics; rather, the name of the game is to sell by whatever tactics are successful. As noted earlier, *Business Week* (January 31, 1977) reported that two-thirds of the managers in two major companies felt pressure to "compromise personal ethics to achieve corporate goals", and that, while nearly 85 percent said they themselves would refuse to "market off-standard and possibly dangerous items," nearly 60 percent considered that "most managers" would not refuse to do so. Over two-thirds stated that "young managers automatically go along with superiors to show loyalty", but almost unanimously the managers considered that business ethics were as good or better than ethics outside of business. Some of the respondents believed the individual was seen as expendable by the company, and therefore would not extend his loyalty to it.

A corporate code of conduct could rectify these views by providing a clear enunciation of the "corporate interest"—its goals, and how they were to be ethically pursued. Such a code would express a recognition of responsibility to multiple groups and the conduct through which that responsibility would be fulfilled. It would express a recognition of the company's continuing role in society and the fact that it honors its responsibilities. It also would specify that each individual manager accepts the responsibilities of his position in the company and is willing to stand liable for his conduct. Finally, the code would help control reprehensible behavior which is not necessarily covered by law.

In sum, as Peter Drucker states in his tome on *Management* (p. 456)—

Morality does not mean preachments. Morality, to have any meaning at all, must be a principle of *action*. It must not be exhortation, sermon, or

good intentions. It must be *practices*. . . . . Management must demonstrate
that it realizes that *integrity* is one absolute requirement of a manager,
the one quality that he has to bring with him and cannot be expected to
acquire later on. And management must demonstrate that it requires the
same integrity of itself.

The company or organization should provide a milieu in which the
best sentiments of its people are translated into action, and which
permits the continuing welfare and development of its personnel.
This requires the development of an *atmosphere* of ethical behavior,
signaled from the top. For small companies, personal example may
be enough. For larger companies, desired behavior needs effective
expression and dissemination in the form of a code of conduct—a
code developed, distributed, and implemented by many managers.

In fact, one of the major benefits of establishing codes of conduct
is the process of discovery and harmonization of interests that occurs
in the participation of many different managers in the formation of
the code. Secretary of Commerce Hodges reported in *The Business
Conscience* that the management of a small company which decided
to develop a code began meeting with about a hundred key employees, only to be amazed

> that everyone in the company had been facing a wide variety of serious
> ethical dilemmas which they had handled case by case without any
> guidance from above. Worse yet, most cases had been resolved in favor of
> the course that would produce the greatest short-run profit.

The employees considered that unethical practices were acceptable in
light of the fact that the company promoted those who made the
largest contributions to profits yet who did not show any serious
concern for ethical considerations; their only option if they didn't
like the situation was to quit. This is unfortunately the view of
managers in a number of company situations, despite the fact that
top management believes it is sending quite different and highly
ethical signals to its managers.

RESPONSIBILITY OF MANAGEMENT

It is the responsibility of management to create an atmosphere of integrity, excellence, performance, and achievement
reflecting ethical standards of behavior—starting at the top and pro-
ceeding through all levels. Mere enunciation in a code is not sufficient; exemplary action is required, as well as an understanding of

the conflicts of loyalties and the grey areas of ethical decisions which individual managers face. Establishment of a code does not resolve problems; it is a guide to the limits of permissible choice. There must be a recognition of the legitimate interests of the various groups affected, both inside and outside the company or organization, who are not represented in the decision making but whose concerns management must take into account. Each manager must understand that his response to these various pressures has significant implications for the company as a whole as well as for his career. The objective of the code, therefore, is to express the collective ethic of the company and to support and assist the individual manager in complying with that ethic.

To facilitate compliance, the code should remove any obstacles to communication and the flow of information among managerial levels. It should facilitate an understanding of what others are doing (rather than just a personal perception of what others are *probably* doing or are likely to do), as well as establish a means of resolving conflicts of interest through guidance from top management levels.

If management is going to claim the right to make certain decisions affecting society, it must show that it is responsible in doing so and that it is willing to live by standards that are higher than the minimum required by law. The alternative is legal standards which are raised to the levels required by ethical conduct. The ensuing regulations would become even more burdensome to management than those which exist today.

Management must also show that it can *enforce* the rules it has adopted. Secretary of Commerce Hodges argued that any "trade association code that doesn't provide for the expulsion of any member violating the code isn't worth the paper it's written on." Violations have to be reported, so the code must make provision for "whistle-blowing" without penalty. Problems may arise here concerning the "encouragement" of "false allegations" and the potential damage to a manager at the hands of a frustrated or disaffected colleague who is simply trying to embarrass him or undercut the system. This potentiality requires that the procedures and channels be as effective as possible in transmitting and assessing information and that penalties and rewards be appropriate.

IBM's ad (*Time*, September 20, 1976), to encourage the formation of codes was aimed at "Restoring Confidence in Business;" and it emphasizes the need to punish violators:

Of all the challenges facing business today, none surpasses the need to put its house in order and regain the public trust.

Public confidence is lower than it has been for many years. In 1966, according to one survey, 55% of Americans had a high level of confidence in business leadership. Today only 16% do.

What has caused this decline?

Many things. But important among them are revelations of corporate kickbacks, bribed officials, illegal political contributions, secret bank accounts and the like.

Some attempts have been made to excuse such misdeeds, saying that 'everybody does it'. This is clearly an evasion of responsibility, even if it were true—which it isn't.

Many companies, including IBM, have rigorous codes of business conduct that they have lived by for years. Codes that clearly spell out the legal and ethical obligations of corporate citizenship.

Many others are working hard toward this objective.

We believe every company should have such a code of conduct. One designed to fit its own situation and its own operations.

We believe that each company should state explicitly the kind of conduct the company expects and the kind of conduct it will not tolerate.

We believe that each company should hold its people to strict observance of that code.

If ever violations are discovered we believe swift action to correct them should be taken—however painful that may be.

Restoring the good name of business deserves the urgent attention of everyone in business today.

It is the best way to assure the survival of business tomorrow.

Indeed, it may be the only way.

EXPECTED OBJECTIONS

A number of objections have been raised to written company codes. A question to be faced early in the dialog is whether or not the publication of a code will invite even closer scrutiny by the public and the press of events happening within the company that might appear to be in violation of the code. Would not outsiders—and even insiders—be induced to say, "Why did this or that happen—since it is in violation of the code? And what have you done about it?" It must be admitted that public awareness of a code may encourage such questions. But open examination of conduct should be welcomed rather than feared. If business is to regain legitimacy and confidence from the people it affects, those people must feel that their interests are being taken into full account and that equity exists at the hands of management. Such questioning also gives management the opportunity to explain its position to the public and therefore to convey how business operates and how it can be expected to respond to given situations. Many a company has argued that it has not been given adequate opportunities to explain itself, and this would produce an opportunity to do so.

A second objection, closely related to the first, is that a confrontation would arise merely out of misperceptions on the part of outsiders, who would object to *apparent* noncompliance with the code when in fact there was full compliance. But again, the corporation has an opportunity to explain itself—before trouble arises, whenever possible, though it is certainly not possible to anticipate all of the different reactions of the various groups to corporate activities.

A third objection is that codes are likely to be seen as "window-dressing" rather than as substantive, making the public even more suspect of the motivations of business than they were before. This is, in my view, a pessimistic response: it implies that public suspicion prevents businesses from doing good. In fact, it is this very suspicion which must be removed, and it is only through the establishment of codes which are implemented and *seen* to be implemented that suspicions can be gradually reduced.

A fourth objection, raised over the past twenty years, is that codes appear to be a "self-condemnation" by the company—a recognition of the validity of criticisms concerning unethical practices. Obviously, where the company has been found to be in violation of law, or where company officials have been found acting either illegally or unethically, promulgation of a code after the fact may appear to be an admission of guilt. But the guilt is already proven; the code is an assertion that the company no longer accepts this kind of behavior and wishes to signal that fact to management and to others. Where the company has been operating ethically, the code can be couched as an expression of long-standing policies and practices which it is now necessary to publicize because of the size of the company and the complexity of lines of communication.

A final objection raised by many within companies concerns surveillance and enforcement procedures. They are concerned about encouraging "tattling" and the disturbances which would arise from it, about incursions on the right of privacy from internal surveillance, and about potential legal suits arising from internal enforcement procedures which might not be seen as acceptable by the courts. These problems can be mitigated by having enforcement procedures and penalties stated clearly in the code—as IBM does, indicating that the penalty is dismissal, and having its managers accept the rules of behavior.

I admit that the establishment of codes may produce new problems. Every solution to a problem tends to raise others. But the problems which business will solve through promulgation of codes of behavior are much more important for its future than those arising from implementation. To conclude otherwise is comparable to arguing that the problems of applying a judicial system are so excruciating that it is better not to have such a system at all.

CHARACTERISTICS OF A CODE

Several characteristics of codes require substantial discussion within the company before an orientation can be agreed upon. They extend from the purposes, through the means of composing the code, to its provisions, and to administration and publication.

Purposes

A number of purposes can be addressed by a code of conduct, and several of them simultaneously. For example, a prime purpose could be a statement of principles which managers are supposed to keep in mind—such as excellence in performance, respect for the individual, the offering of a "fair deal," the provision of "an honest day's work for an honest day's pay," the extension of equal opportunity to all, the maintenance of integrity and honesty, and behavior which is above what the law requires. Though it may not be enough to enunciate such principles and leave it at that, their enunciation sets the stage for the rest of the code provisions.

Other purposes depend on whether the code is to be a set of internal guidelines or to constitute specific rules for managerial behavior. Is management to set an example for others in the company, or is the code applicable throughout all levels of company personnel?

Still another purpose of the code would be to achieve public recognition for the orientation of the company as expressed in the code, and to gain a favorable response from potential customers, suppliers, governments, or the community. This purpose presumes publication and wide dissemination of the code. A code is "internal" if addressed only to those within a company. If addressed to the public—saying, in effect, "this is who we are and how we act"—or to potential customers or the local community, then outsiders know what to expect in terms of management's or members' behavior. These different purposes will affect the way in which the code is written and presented.

Code Objectives

Specific code objectives relate to what managers (or workers or association members) are to do in pursuit of the overall company goals. For example, one objective might be to provide an opportunity for creative work, opening channels for individual development, expression, and initiative. Another might be to promote a service orientation on the part of management both within the company and in the community. Related to this might be the objective of encouraging managers to seek ways in which the company as a whole could make contributions to community life. A further objective might be to promote leadership on the part of management. It can be argued that not all managers are leaders—at least not in the same way—but leadership is not always active or initiatory; leadership of a passive sort can also be important, such as an individual meeting his responsibilities and fulfilling corporate responsibilities in such a way that others emulate him.

Finally, the code should elicit a higher quality of performance from those to whom it is addressed, in the sense that performance is, as Drucker states, "morality in action." Performance which achieves specific objectives, without also doing it in acceptable ways, is not acceptable performance.

Procedures for Composition of the Code

The selection of purposes and objectives and the specific provisions to support these goals will be affected by the process of discussion and by who has responsibility for writing the code. Some companies have given this responsibility to Board members; others give it to the public relations department, the legal department, or the personnel department. Some companies have formed *ad hoc* committees composed of officials of several different departments and even overseas affiliates, in order to draw on a full range of views. One can almost tell from the way a code is written and presented which procedure was employed. Thus, the procedure itself signals some of the intent of the company. The orientation of the code is also affected by the level of personnel involved in the dialogue—whether from the board of directors, top management, or sub-management levels. The very numbers of persons involved will affect the orientation of the code, its provisions, and its acceptability or response within the company. Whether those who are involved are wholly inside the company or include some outsiders will also affect the orientation of the code. Therefore, a conscious decision should be made about procedures to be employed, in the light of the desired objectives.

The code should be a "living document," accommodating revisions or addenda when appropriate. They signal to the persons involved that the code is responsive to changes in orientation or social values and to changes in the company or association itself.

Finally, the actual composition of the code and the writing style give important signals to readers about its nature and orientation. Some codes, for example, have a chatty style which indicates that the code is a dialogue among family members who understand each other but simply need a little reinforcement. Others are legalistic in form and language, with detachable documents recording acceptances which are put in personnel files. Some codes are couched in the form of the "ten commandments." Still others are written in persuasive styles, indicating that everything may not be understood by those who are to comply, and that a careful and considered response is necessary but not a "legally binding" one. An assessment of the implications of these different styles is required if management is to achieve its objectives.

Provisions

The first decision about the provisions themselves is whether they should be specific or general, simple or detailed, guidelines or rules. This decision will depend again on the purposes and objectives indicated above and whether there is a juridicial orientation to the code, as distinct from a hortatory orientation.

Regardless of orientation, an initial provision in most codes is a declaration of adherence to "high ethical principles" and an assertion that managers are to act in ways above what is required by law. There is usually also a provision which stipulates that managers are to comply with all relevant laws, and that this constitutes *minimum* behavior. When a manager is in doubt, he is frequently encouraged to consult with legal counsel in the company so as to obtain proper guidance and, incidentally, to cover himself if the act is questioned later.

Provisions are often included relating to conflicts of interests between a manager's personal interests and those of the company, requiring him to avoid such conflicts or to report them for resolution in case they do arise. He is often enjoined from using "inside information" in ways which would appear detrimental to others associated with the company.

Other provisions relate to activities inside and outside the company; they are included according to the priorities of management and the kinds of activities in which the association or company is engaged. Some of these provisions are suggested by the following subjects:

customer relations
political participation and contributions
side payments to customers or suppliers
individual personnel relations
product protection, safety, packaging, labeling, and quality
advertising—accuracy, advocacy, institutional
consumer promotions
industry leadership
service to employees
community relations and contributions
industrial espionage
supplier relations
propietary information and information disclosure
protection of company property
accounting for company funds
environmental protection
relations with the news media
responsibility for adherence to the code—personal and observance
    by others
penalties for non-compliance

Whether a particular provision is included and how it should be expressed is obviously a matter for each company or association; the level of detail depends on the nature of operations. For example, the Bank of America has a code which is almost wholly related to information disclosure, with numerous provisions relating to voluntary openness about information which customers and others have a need to know: the provision of relevant information to multiple constituencies, as the need is determined; promptness of reply to information requests; protection of privacy and confidentiality; non–disclosure of information to competitors; and avoidance of the use of subjective information where it is not clearly labeled as such or where it could be mistaken for company policy or company-based information. Such detailed provisions obviously reflect the fact that the firm is a bank, where inquiries by the public or government are likely to be frequent and sometimes delicate.

Dissemination of the Code

Expectations about the nature and strength of response to the code are signaled finally by the method of dissemination. For example, if the code is transmitted to managers from the board, the chairman of the board, or the president of the company, it has a stature and significance greater than if transmitted from any lower level. Acceptance by signature annually, or at some periodic interval, stresses that the code is current and binding.

The code has a different effect if dissemination is limited to certain levels within the company—if it is distributed to management and not to employees, for example, or to full time employees but not to part-time workers.

The code is also different in its effect if it is published and widely disseminated, or held privately within the company.

Finally, the intent of the code is conveyed in the covering letter—whether condemnatory of past behavior, or exhortative of good behavior with compliments for past excellence.

Nothing can substitute in the strength of communication for the exemplary behavior of the CEO and other top managers. When the actions of top management are seen as carrying out the intent of the code, that intent is most effectively expressed.

Administration of the Code

The code is merely a piece of paper with words on it if there are no penalties for non-compliance. Indeed, it is probably worse to have a code which is known to be unenforced or unenforceable—or from which some are exempted—than to have no code at all. This is the problem with the honor systems in various educational institutions which are recognized increasingly as inapplicable and can be violated with impunity.

Several difficult problems exist in the administration of codes. In order to alleviate some of these problems, it is probably best to establish a "conduct committee" or ombudsman, to which people would report on their problems and who in turn would report to a superior. Consideration should be given to establishing the conduct committee or ombudsman at a level where peers evaluate an individual's activities, rather than people far up the supervisory line. Surveillance and enforcement have the necessary internal purpose of maintaining the validity of the code and establishing a high morale within the company or association. They have the external purpose of precluding regulation by community or governmental authorities, by demonstrating compliance with internal rules. Unless such compliance is demonstrated through enforcement, it is likely that the rules will be set through laws, or that mechanisms will be established for outside enforcement, as in the case of some medical activities.

Problems in administration arise from the process of surveillance itself. Can personnel be expected to report activities which they engage in themselves or which others engage in that might be outside of the limits of acceptability? Or is it necessary to have an internal policing mechanism? Both procedures raise difficult questions, but no worse than those faced by everyone in society. Note the contradictory demands of parents that children "tell the truth" but not "tattle." Within the area of surveillance, probably the most difficult exercise is whistle-blowing, but it is necessary to bring non-compliance to the surface, to say nothing of exposing illegal or fraudulent activities. Protection must be provided within the code for those who expose illegitimate activities.

Procedures for surveillance and judgment must include the application of penalties. A method is required to make the penalty "fit the crime," so that all members believe that justice is done. Given the difficulties of any such internal judicial process, however, procedures must also be available for appeal—at least within the company; additional consideration must be given to the overlapping of external judicial procedures and internal ones.

There is also the matter of whether enforcement is to be kept private and secret, or if not, the extent to which the final decision and various aspects of the case are to be made public. Obviously, most companies would prefer to keep such problems to themselves, but this impinges on public regard of the code as being implemented appropriately—which is of course one objective in restoring public confidence. In any case, the removal of an official from a visible position in the company will raise questions to which some response is likely to be required.

Finally, there are bound to be differences in interpretations of the various provisions, necessitating a procedure for clarification and for determination of appropriate judgment. This can follow precedent or prior judgment, counsel with legal officials, or the judgment of an ombudsman or conduct committee, as suggested above.

CONCLUSIONS

A growing number of companies and associations are developing and promulgating codes of conduct. The issue of codes has been raised to the international level concerning the activities of transnational corporations, where intergovernmental groups are attempting to establish alternatives to international legal arrangements. The revelation of bribes and illicit payments to various intermediaries in governmental sales and investment projects internationally has raised questions about appropriate company behavior and colored all company activities. Rather than wait for others to develop codes of appropriate behavior, it behooves business to look at itself and decide how it needs to behave. Given the differences among companies and their situations, no generalized code for business as a whole is likely to be applicable. It may be that even industry-wide codes would probably not be specific enough. Each company and association needs to assess its own problems in this regard and its responses to the increasingly apparent impact of their activities on the interests of others. The process of developing and promulgating a code will itself sharpen the realization of management's responsibilities and possibly reduce government interference in the freedom of enterprise.

DISCUSSION QUESTIONS

1. Does my company or association need a code of conduct? For what purposes?
2. Why do we have to set rules, rather than letting all personnel simply abide by the rules of decency and fair play?
3. What are the risks of having a code?—or of not having one? How should we make these tradeoffs?
4. Is it likely that company codes will become mandated by Congress? Or will it mandate enforcement of existing company codes?
5. Should outside (local or national or international) community officials be drawn into the formation or implementation of a company or association code?

SUGGESTED READINGS

Hammaker, P. M., A. B. Horniman, and L. T. Rader. *Standards of Conduct in Business.* Charlottesville, Va.: University of Virginia, Center for Study of Applied Ethics, Graduate School of Business Administration, 1977.

Hill, Ivan (ed.). *The Ethical Basis of Economic Freedom.* Washington: American Viewpoint, Inc., Part Four.

Hodges, L. H. *The Business Conscience.* Englewood Cliffs, N.J.: Prentice-Hall, Chaps. 12–14.
Opinion Research Corporation. *Codes of Ethics in Corporations and Trade Associations,* 1979.

Examples of Codes

Bank of America Corporation. *Voluntary Disclosure Code.*
Caterpillar Tractor Company. *A Code of Worldwide Business Conduct.*
Eli Lilly Company. *Guidelines of Company Policy.*
Government Accounting Office. *Ethics Code.*
IBM. *Business Conduct Guidelines.*
Xerox. *An Understanding.*

Chapter 10

Values vs. Numerical Goals

In an assessment of Japan's recent economic development, the Director-General of Japan's Economic Planning Agency, Tokusakuro Kasaka, concluded, "We have only lived for numbers, and they have brought us to a dead end" (*Vision*, March 1979). His point was *not* that Japan relied on numbers to tell what was happening but that it used them to tell where they ought to be going. Numbers are valueless in the sense of containing an ethical quality in and of themselves. *More* steel or *more* clothes are not necessarily "good things." Yet, since the U.S., Japan, and Germany are the only three countries of the world which produce voluminous statistics and data for use in the sciences and social sciences, and since they are the most advanced, aggressive, and innovative of countries, there must be something good about such numerical measurements.

I am not attacking quantification. What I wish to discuss is the *substitution* of numbers (quantification) for judgment in decision making—the substitution of numbers for responsibility—as in the case of their use as goals rather than indicators of certain aspects of performance.

The issue is illustrated in an editorial entitled, "IQ Testers Need Heads Examined," which appeared in a European business magazine. It reports that a London-based company, on the recommendation of a social psychologist, decided to fix the salaries of their workers in accordance with the results of intelligence tests. Of the total of 500 workers in the company, 364 refused to be tested. They were in fact smarter than the social psychologist, the editors commented, because they had figured out that if one had a low score, his salary would be cut; if the score was exceedingly high, he would be fired. The editors proceeded to argue that payment according to level of intelligence would be extremely unfair, since pay must also have something to do with ability and willingness to work. The society would be turned upside down, otherwise, since the hundreds of business leaders who had fought their way to the top without great brain power would have to be removed or have their salaries cut. Finally they queried, who would we get to fill most of our responsible positions if they required extreme intelligence?

This incident points up the effects of substituting numbers for judgment. Someone must judge the *value* of an individual's effort in a company, and no numerical testing can do so.

DRIVE FOR QUANTIFICATION

Still, there is a strong drive in the United States to use quantification as the basis *and* the procedure for decision making. This orientation is supported by the numerous disciplines based on measurements—econometrics, sociometrics, psychometrics, polyscimetrics, even historimetrics—as well as the variety of quantitative methods applied to such areas as operations research for business decision making. Application of scientific methods to the setting of goals is contrary to the nature of social problems. These issues require subjective judgments, based on other than numerical systems of value.

The social sciences are so subjective and numerically indefinite that Norbert Weiner, the father of cybernetics (the theoretical basis of computers), concluded that they were "one-digit" sciences—if science at all. That is, they could not appropriately be extended beyond one meaningful digit to the left—one million, one billion, and so forth—and certainly not into decimal places. Their measurements are so imprecise and the impact of time is so great that no series of data over time is homogeneous. The data are not comparable, so only gross estimates—or as *Time* magazine used to call them, "guesstimates"—are possible.

Despite this limitation, policy makers seek increasingly to maximize a quantity or achieve a given number—to seek "more" of something, according to a numerical scale. For example, the gross national product (GNP) is the measure of our prosperity—and presumably the measure of our happiness. Since total personal income in current dollars has increased nearly five-fold in the past twenty years, we should now be five times happier! Per capita income has increased nearly four times, so taking inflation into account, we are still twice as well off in real terms, on the average, as we were in 1960. But are we twice as happy now? Will we be twice again as happy in 1999?

GNP has become such a key to determining success that we rate Presidential performance based on whether the level of GNP is appropriate and its rate of growth satisfactory. President Kennedy, in the early days of his tenure, was reported as having assumed responsibility for "running the country" by raising the GNP. Since that time, every President has had to declare that he could raise GNP—and cut unemployment—to a satisfactory numerical level. Our measurement for "winning" the Vietnam war was the body count. We determine the success of welfare programs by the numbers of people who are no longer on the roles, regardless of how they are treated or who *should* be covered; of rehabilitation programs according to the numbers of those "rehabilitated" within a given budget, irrespective of those who were "too expensive" to rehabilitate. Treatment of the aged in retirement homes is measured according to the number of calories and variety of food offered, regardless of whether it is needed or wanted. Minority hiring is done according to quotas. Corporate goals are set in terms of monetary profits. The Boy Scouts of America was recently embarrassed by the revelation that Scoutmasters were signing up new members, without concern for their staying with the group, simply to meet membership targets in a national drive. Churches still consider increasing their membership a measure of success; yet Christ limited his inner circle to twelve.

PROBLEMS IN QUANTIFICATION

There are serious problems with quantification—difficulties with measurement itself in the social sciences, and some alarming implications in use of numbers—that extend into the arena of corporate social responsibility.

The problems of measurement relate to *what* is to be measured, *how* to measure it, how to obtain the data, and the reliability of data. Ironically, each of these questions can be answered only by subjective judgments. *What* should be measured in order to determine GNP, for example? Why are only items with prices included? We have determined what to measure according to the ability to gauge value in money prices. Similarly, in the area of pollution control, the desired level of cleanness of air or water is determined by our ability to measure it. The more precise the measuring devices become, the more stringent the standards—without regard for whether one level of cleanliness is more desirable from multiple (cost/benefit) standpoints than another. Absolutely "pure" distilled water is probably not very good for you, since it would not have the trace minerals and other substances which are valuable to the body. How much of these elements are desirable we do not yet know.

The composition of the GNP is based on the assumption that more material goods provide happiness. However, more of each thing that is in the GNP is not necessarily better, nor will it necessarily bring happiness. The value of dental services is included; must we conclude that, since more tooth decay would mean more use of such services and would increase the GNP, we would be happier? Greater consumption of gasoline means an increase in GNP, even if it is consumed in frustratingly long traffic lines. Time spent reading a book or listening to music is not included in GNP, yet does that not add to our happiness? Educational expenses are included, but they merely replace one generation by the next, in a manner similar to depreciation. *Should* we count only what one generation learns above that of the previous one? If, in fact, we *deducted* the expenses of merely "staying even" with ourselves year to year, we would have a much better measure of the additions to our growth or happiness. But this would substantially reduce the level of GNP, which statistically we would not want to do.

How should we measure the items with which we are truly concerned? How do we obtain the data? It has been said, about the Bureau of the Census, that the statisticians who manipulate the data would quit their jobs if they knew how the data were collected; the census takers, likewise, would quit obtaining samples if they knew how the statisticians manipulated the data. The point is that virtually all data are based on samples, necessarily imperfect and reflect someone's judgment, and in handling the data, errors are frequently made which seriously affect policies based on the numbers—as in the case of the shift in monetary policy in October 1979, when the money supply was erroneously reported as significantly higher than it really was, causing consternation among policy-makers.

There is great doubt about the reliability of data obtained in the social sciences. For example, Princeton professor Oscar Morganstern (co-author with the great mathematician von Neumann of *The Theory of Games and Economic Behavior*) concluded on the basis of a ten-year study that the data on the gold movements in the nineteenth century were grossly in error. Yet considerable international theory is based on that erroneous data, and hence is itself grossly in error. Similarly, an economic advisor to President Kennedy was provided some data on a particularly important event and was asked to explain how it had occurred. He did so, working overnight on the data to be able to explain the next morning to the President what the statistical causation was. When he returned to his office the next afternoon he found new information to the effect that the event had not occurred. He then had to revise his interpretation of the data to show *why* it had *not* happened.

One of the greatest errors we make in business is to assume that an accountant is telling the truth. It is not easy for him to be perfectly accurate, yet we *assume* the figures are right when they are written down. We know from the controversy over FASB rulings that numbers do not always reflect reality. It seems that the more people who accept a given number, once printed, the more "accurate" it becomes. General acceptance tends to give validity even to numbers.

The very process of quantification has some insidious implications. The first is that quantification becomes a substitute for thinking; more is seen automatically as better than less. All one needs to do is plug in the data, and out comes the solution. Such a method shifts the matter of thinking into design of the model by which the data are processed. The structure of that model becomes of primary importance; the inputs of reliable data are secondary! One gets, as the standard comment on computers goes, "garbage in, garbage out."

The impact of numerical goals on decision making is to reduce individual responsibility and the decision-making *ability* of the manager. He is now *required* to do whatever achieves the numerical objective: so much output, so many clients visited, so much in sales, profit targets, and so forth—without (unassessed) tradeoffs in regard to quality, service, etc.—or the manner in which goals are accomplished. At the extreme, this can become as absurd as the situation observed in the Soviet Union, where physical output was the only goal; to maximize production of shoes (and get his bonus), a plant manager produced all *left* shoes, and only in size 11E. Decision makers in a *free* society must take other than quantitative factors into account and be permitted to make mistakes. Strictly numerical goals reflect a bureaucratic management orientation that is increasingly adverse to risk, leaning towards the certainty and security of quantitative targets without regard or responsibility for the qualitative aspects. The result is also a reduction of creativity.

Creativity is left for the one who *designs* the decision model. Decision makers, using the model, merely follow plan. But the trouble with models for decision making is that they are constructed with little awareness of value implications. In his lectures on the relation of cybernetics to religion, Norbert Weiner explains that God, when He picked up the golem (in Jewish folklore, the blob of earth used to make man) had to have in mind a complete design for a system; otherwise, He would not have been able to fit man into his environment. Not to understand the full implications of the decision model, as well as the methods of data collection, is not to understand the implications of solutions which result.

DESIRABILITY OF MORE

"More" is *not* always "better." It depends! It depends on the effects of the more and how the more is obtained. More employment is not necessarily better; it depends on what people are doing. More goods and services are not necessarily better; it depends on what kinds of goods and services are produced. Is more sugar and more candy better, indefinitely? I don't even need to ask about the desirability of more mind–bending or body–debilitating drugs. More is also not always better, depending on for whom it is intended and the use to which it will be put. There is a question, therefore, of the distribution of the more. Is more housing better? More hotels? Or do we need to ask if old people will be displaced by new high-rise condominiums? Is more coal better, regardless of the effects of strip mining? And who bears the social and environmental costs? None of these questions can be decided apart from a series of subjective valuations.

Quantification is now invading the area of business' social responsibility. The exercise called "social auditing" has as its objective the numerical determination of when and how a company has met its social responsibilities, so someone can prove that the job has been done. Once again, this is an effort to substitute numbers for thinking. Responsibility for acting acceptably is being substituted by a model of "acceptable behavior" based on numbers. It need not be this way. Chase Manhattan Bank has asked its affiliates around the world to design appropriate social responsibility programs, which will be discussed with headquarters; there is no stipulation for mere number counting in minority hiring, community giving, and the like.

QUANTIFICATION OF VALUES

I am trying to emphasize that values are not quantifiable. They are not scientific; they are not inputs; neither can they be measured. Efficiency criteria related to inputs and outputs are simply not applicable to the values which of necessity underlie goal setting. No data system or analysis, however sophisticated, can cope with the profound decisions concerning which groups within society *should* benefit from what types of actions. These decisions require value judgments.

The criteria of acceptability of any institution, including business, are shaped in terms of fundamental values—truth, equality, justice, freedom, quality of life, and so on. None of these are quantifiable. Yet in the U.S. we increasingly rely on quantities to determine if we have succeeded. In doing so, we have seriously altered our judgment. The economic criteria for efficiency, productivity, and business success are almost always quantified. Some economists have gone so far as to argue, "if you can't quantify it, it is not economics." The discipline has moved that way, and so has business. In the process, a tendency has arisen to exclude all non-quantifiable criteria. The quantities which make sense in present day economics are those which have to do with volumes of production, output, prices, cost, incomes, and so forth. They lead to calculations of costs and benefits, but only those which are measurable.

But not one criterion for what ultimately is sought in a society is quantifiable—not even "progress." We assume that an increase in real GNP is good—always good. The press, the President, economists, and businessmen all say so—but by what criteria? Why is an increase in GNP always better? Does the composition of GNP make no difference? Is it always possible to raise GNP? I can give you a formula which is certain to raise GNP—a GNP comprised only of outputs without consideration for inputs or sources of inputs: run down the environment, rape nature, and don't deduct replacement of equipment; sure enough, GNP will increase! If you ran your business that way, it would be short-lived. One runs a business with the idea of *continuing* it, which means counting the cost of all inputs and considering the *future*. Nobody is responsible, however, for making sure that GNP is not obtained at excessive social cost. No such calculation is made. We increase GNP at costs which do not reflect depreciation of the environment.

Neither does GNP include measures of the real value of items composing it. Is it not possible for one GNP to be better than another of the same monetary value in reflecting or meeting the goals of society? Economists make no such calculations. Is it not possible for one GNP to be better distributed in terms of social goals than another? Yet, GNP says nothing about that. It is assumed that as a country gets wealthier, *all* people are better off. It is assumed that not as many people starve to death, and fewer have to go without clothes or food simply because GNP is higher. That assumption is not reliable. *More* GNP is *not* necessarily better than a lower, but *different*, GNP.

VALUE OF MORE

Let's put this matter in the context of company operations. Is more production better than less? More sales better than less? More profits better than less? For the company, perhaps! It really depends on how they are made. Quantification is very attractive, for it makes it easy to ignore value judgments. I used to teach international business at the American Management Association in New York. I remember one manager getting frustrated by my analysis of the complex forces affecting the international balance of payments. He finally said, "Please! Stop telling us what all these different figures mean and give me *the* figure for the *deficit*. I just want to know how big it is." But it didn't really matter *what* I said it was, for unless he knew what it *meant* underneath and what the composition of the payments meant to business, he couldn't really understand. A $6 billion deficit may be a lot easier to handle than a $3 billion deficit—depending on how it occurred, the conditions emerging internationally, and who is holding dollars overseas. Quantification appears to relieve us of the need for assessment of what's happening beneath the numbers and of making value judgments about where we should be going.

GOALS AS QUANTITIES

Ask yourself how to quantify variables which make up pleasure, which presumably is a goal. How do you quantify happiness? How do you measure severity of crime? Less crime is better than more, right? Always! How about those figures that come from the police: "We have less crime in our city than in the past decade." But do you know *what* they were measuring? Did they tell you there is a shift away from petty theft, and an increase of rape and assault? How many purse snatchings equal a murder? Numbers will fool you; we have got to look behind them.

What are the factors by which one can measure love? Friendship? Respect? Reverence? Diligence? How does one quantify equity or justice? "The quality of mercy is not strain'd," said Portia in the *Merchant of Venice*. What are the input–output criteria for the exercise of love or friendship? What is the maximum output of love that one can achieve with minimum input? On the contrary, all religions clearly assert that the expression of love requires maximum *in*put, and that the "output" or return will be appropriate, but uncertain in nature or volume. Love is *in*efficient by numerical measures. The value foundations of a society are simply not measurable, yet they form our *goals*!

Neither computer programs, decision models, nor sociometrics of any type will answer the questions we face in life concerning fulfillment of our commitments in marriage, the appropriate community involvement, the time tradeoffs between job and family, whether and when to locate our parents in a home for the elderly, how much to give to the church or other charities, when it is acceptable to lie, what is "an honest day's work for an honest day's pay," or *how* to pursue income or profit.

In addressing these issues, one should avoid the confusion we have previously discussed that the score is the *reason* for the game. The score is *not* the reason for the game. The score says nothing of the worth or objective of a game in a community or society—not even its value to the spectators (with the exception of the gamblers). The score says nothing of how the game was played, of the impact on the players, or whether they will happily return to play again. However, the *emphasis* we have placed on the score—on quantification—has shifted our attention almost exclusively to winning and away from the playing and the recreational purpose of games.

Likewise, as we previously discussed, profit is not the *reason* for business nor does the existence of profit necessarily indicate that the company is doing a "good" job—unless *all* the conditions under which profit was made were also ethically acceptable. Profit says nothing about the objectives of a business or the company's worth to society. It says nothing about how the profit was earned, nor the impact of the business on the people involved. When profit becomes the *sole* objective, it is sought by any means—as it was in the case of the small group of bond traders at Chase Manhattan who made fraudulent entries in their accounts in order to reach the numerical targets set by top management. Their excuse? They believed that the targets had to be met.

Neither is material success the reason for living. It is a long stretch of the imagination to think that God picked up the golem to form man for the purpose of his achieving material success—especially since He had already created the materials which man would have available. Material success is only one of the many scores in life. But as William James said years ago, we have made material success into an illness, and the cash expression of it has become the national disease. As I mentioned earlier, I consider this cash expression of success—rather than the mere creation of money or government spending alone— a cause of the present inflation in the U.S. Inflation is the result of groups and individuals with power in the society attempting to shift the income distribution in their favor by raising prices or wages. The inability to succeed in this effort creates not only more inflation but continued frustration, which is in turn producing great social malaise.

PLACE OF MATERIALISM

There is nothing wrong with materialism—if it is secondary! That is, secondary to honesty, to love, to companionship, to equity, and justice. If it comes first, it leads to various forms of corruption, such as the dipping of company officials into corporate slush funds. Companies created slush funds for illicit payments in the U.S. and abroad; then those in charge of them found it convenient to divert some of the funds into their own pockets. As former Governor Luther Hodges used to say, "If you teach a man to steal for you, he will steal from you." Corruption for the purpose of material gain is not limited to business, of course. There is cheating in universities for the purpose of getting into graduate schools—so that in the long run one's material advance can be greater; there is falsification of research on the part of professors and scientists for the purpose of achieving reputations and, therefore, greater material success.

But if we look to the Old Testament and to many other religions, we will find that material success was once considered a reward for practicing a *good* life. The truly good life requires commitment and dedication to something greater than the self, and sometimes a sacrifice of material gain.

INDIVIDUAL RESPONSIBILITY

The answer to the question of how one relegates material success to a secondary position comes from within—from one's personal sense of values. These cannot be taught by professors, nor should they be. University professors can only elucidate values, and the best way they can teach is to provide appropriate role models by their own behavior—showing high levels of responsibility to students and the university, a commitment to seek the truth, and dedication to high values. One's own values are learned mostly at home, before entering the first grade; they are then tested continuously through school and in one's career. The contribution of a university faculty is to help expand one's information and acquire the knowledge of how to use it, and to provide a community within which values are expressed and absorbed. Obviously, different value systems are represented by different professors, and students have the opportunity to reinforce their own or adopt new ones. But professors cannot *teach* values: in fact, the verb "to teach" is erroneously classed as a transitive verb. A teacher cannot "teach" as one can "throw" a ball; he can only open doors; the student must walk through to assume the responsibility for learning. Neither can professors *teach* wisdom and judgment. These are acquired only through experience and observation, through exercising one's values in the various decisions of life. The value system each person has is *the* most necessary and significant ingredient of decision making, for it overrides and undergirds all else. Values are what we live *by* and die *for*. Unfortunately, values are not what we seem to *live for*. That seems to reside in quantities—more power, more status, more profit, more goods. I have never heard any one say, "I would lay down my life for a Cadillac." We *live* for material success, and *die* for values.

Happiness, however, is not necessarily achieved by an increase in material things. They are often an obstacle—but only because we do not have our values straight. *Enforced* poverty is certainly a curse; but even so, happiness is not reserved for the rich. Happiness is achieved by fulfillment of the social values and personal virtues, and these can be measured only internally, by one's self, with the encouragement of social recognition and reinforcement.

In conclusion, let me put forward two maxims which I consider useful. One comes from the scientific realm and the other from the mystical. With Albert Einstein, I believe that these two realms can be reconciled, and that their reconciliation should be the goal of science. The scientific maxim comes from the *Journal of Irreproducible Results*, which includes articles by scientists who take their methodologies a little less seriously than most. The maxim: "If a project is not worth doing at all, it is not worth doing well."

A graduate student who intended to write a dissertation showing that everything could be quantified asked me to chair his Ph.D. thesis committee. When I explained to him that he had chosen the wrong individual, and that such an exercise was not my "bag," he insisted he still wanted me to participate because if he could get the thesis by me, he knew it would be solid. I asked him why he wanted to quantify everything, and he replied that it would make decision making easy because one would simply compare the quantities. Knowing he was married, I asked him if he could quantify love. He assured me he could, to which I replied, "I would be interested in your wife's response when you tell her how much you love her. Whatever you say, I am sure it will not be enough." Suffice it to say, after several attempts, he abandoned the thesis.

The *methods* employed in science do not validate the *worth* of the project, and their progressive refinement into more sophisticated (quantified) techniques will not necessarily add to the project's value. The worth of a research project or business comes from the goals which it serves and its impact on those affected; the performance can be weighed only against a value system.

The second maxim comes from Carlos Casteneda's record of the mystical, but often clearly practical, *Teachings of Don Juan*. On asking for some criterion to guide his life, Carlos was advised by Don Juan, "If you have a choice among the roads of life, take the one with heart."

DISCUSSION QUESTIONS

1. What is the appeal of quantification of ends and means in your business?
   a. Is it a defensible appeal?
   b. Can that desire be met by other means?
2. What is the difference in quantification of goals and quantification of means? Should they be separated?
3. At what level of refinement is quantification appropriate—as, for example, in clean air and water standards? In processing I.R.S. audits? In setting sales or profit targets?
4. If our major life decisions cannot be quantified, how can we make sound decisions? Of what *use* is quantification?

SELECTED READINGS

Backman, Jules (ed.), *Social Responsibility and Accountability*. New York: New York University Press, 1975, Chaps. 4-7.

Beckerman, W. *In Defence of Economic Growth*. London: Jonathan Cape, 1974.

Meadows, D. L. (ed.), *Alternatives to Growth/I*. Cambridge, Mass.: Ballinger, 1977.

Weiner, Norbert. *God and Golem*. Boston: MIT Press, 1964.

Chapter 11

The Future as Past and Present

The manager who is serving his company well is investing now for two decades hence—for the year 2000 and beyond. What will the situation be then? What will be expected of business? The second question is easier to answer: business will be expected to make acceptable contributions to many more facets of life than material growth or than simple expansion of production or GNP. Much greater attention will be given to the *use* of various inputs, their re-use, their improvement, and to the composition of output. Managing will, therefore, become much more complex, and managers will be expected to help develop the "whole" man or woman associated with the company. The manager will be looked to as a steward and a "statesman" in the sense of responding to, though not setting priorities for, community and national needs and goals.

The physical and material aspects of life in the twenty-first century will be considerably more advanced and enjoyable than they are now—barring catastrophe and assuming a continuing flow of invention and discovery. If the past two decades are a pattern at all, we

This chapter is based on a paper presented at a symposium entitled "Working in the 21st Century," co-sponsored by The Colgate Darden Graduate School of Business Administration (University of Virginia) and The Wharton School (University of Pennsylvania) and funded by Philip Morris Incorporated. The conference papers have been published in book form by John Wiley & Sons, Inc.

can expect a doubling of the real standard of living for the average American. It is not clear, however, that this increase will be distributed equitably or that people will be any happier then they are today. Contrary to the message of advertising, happiness does not come in packages.

We are likely to face a series of complex problems that are felt even more critically because of the pressures of living more closely together. It is questionable whether technical nostrums will be any more able than they are today to provide us with acceptable resolutions. Solutions will require political will based on the underlying values of society. For example, we will undoubtedly have more deadly and extensive weaponry with which to protect ourselves; from whence will come the will to seek disarmament?

Pressing problems will arise in the broader social and political arenas where the manager will be expected to play a significant role as advisor and implementor. The challenges of the twenty-first century are likely to be the same as those which face us today and which have faced most civilizations in the past, though in different degrees. Some challenges have been partially met, but their aspects diverge rather than converge to a neat solution. They are problems for which any "solution" can come unstuck with a shift in values, power relations, or environment. Without trying to be exhaustive or to characterize each of them in detail, let us note seventeen which seem certain to demand the attention of business in the twenty-first century. Each holds within it an opposite or a tradeoff which makes the choices difficult. The future will be described by our responses.

1. Achieving global *unity* with desired cultural *diversity*. This translates into peace with autonomy, or the development of a feeling of community with sufficient individualism to permit each person to seek his own destiny. It also raises the problem of specialization, which requires a meshing of talents yet with a degree of self-reliance.

2. *Motivating* people to produce necessary and desirable goods and services, without stimulating *greed* and self-serving activities only. This raises the question of how to relegate materialism to a second-order priority while keeping its motivating force.

3. Achieving a *competitive*, yet *cooperative*, society—maintaining the dynamism which comes from competition, while not pulling the system apart. This requires a cooperative effort toward mutual goals that permits progress rather than stagnation.

4. Permitting effective *opposition* while maintaining social and political *cohesion*. How can we maintain the system while encouraging dissent, or permit adversary positions while mobilizing groups to face mutual problems?

5. Gaining adequate and appropriate *production* with an acceptable *distribution of the benefits*, both income and happiness. This requires resolution of the problem of motivation and its conflict with the principle of equality. Productivity needs to be increased while at the same time permitting greater participation on the part of those involved, without forcing some to bear the burdens of others. The goods needed for mass consumption should be produced and available, without leveling all to the same living standard.

6. Achieving *order*—political, economic, and social—with *flexibility*. Order must be flexible so as not to break with evolutionary change. This raises the questions of how to achieve stability with progress—and what, in fact, is progress.

7. Providing increasingly sophisticated *opportunities* for labor, with greater responsibility, while maintaining *respect* for all forms and sources of labor. What is the role of labor in life, and how can it be utilized without making it a commodity and thereby dictating to the laborer his place in society? What can be done about discrimination in employment?

8. Achieving *technological advance* without destruction of the *culture*. In other words, what is the proper use of technology and its relationhip to man's purpose in work.

9. Gaining social and geographic *mobility* while maintaining desired community *values*. What is the role of the family and its relationship to the community? What are its responsibilities to the extended family and to others within the community? The structure of the community is likely to change, with new forms of urbanization and satellite towns. These changes will affect the family's role of transmitting culture from one generation to another, and of providing stability while encouraging evolutionary change in the individual.

10. Assuming the *responsibilities of government* while maintaining an adequate role for *private initiative*. This raises questions about the impact of regulations for social purposes versus private interests, and the problem of bureaucratic rigidity in decision-making compared to the responsiveness of market decisions. There are also the problems of how to maintain democracy based on adequate information while protecting one's privacy. Further, individual participation alters the

level of government responsible for a social or economic issue; greater local responsibility gains participation of affected groups but raises the problem of how to maintain nationwide equality of treatment.

11. Achieving personal *freedom* while developing social *responsibility*. What should be the constraints on individualism for the purpose of social equity in development? How should we determine the responsibility of the individual in specific cases; how retrieve personalities which have become antisocial (e.g., use of behavior modification techniques)?

12. Achieving *justice* with *mercy* in political, economic, social and juridical matters. In other words, how to achieve an equitable society.

13. Commanding the *resources* of nature while maintaining the appropriate *integration* of man with his environment. How free is man to alter the environment? Or is he, in fact, evolving over the long term under rather tight constraints from his environment? Is his ability to command nature somewhat illusory? Is *direction* more realistic than *control*?

14. *Protecting* the society while maintaining *privacy* of the individual. This raises questions about security as well as information needs in a more complex and interdependent society.

15. Permitting the *nationalism* required to build communities without the destruction of necessary sentiments and activities supporting *internationalism*. How can we gain cohesion in smaller groups without increasing discrimination against "foreigners"? On a socio-psychological or religious plane, the problem is how to expand fraternal love while maintaining the openness to foster its wider expression.

16. Encouraging individual achievement in the *present* without holding the *future* hostage. How can we integrate the needs of future generations into the decision-making criteria of the present? The market does not respond to *future* demands— only demands which have taken the future into account in their formulation. A means is needed, therefore, of balancing future and present needs and desires so that decision makers have adequate resources to promote the continued improvement of life.

17. Accelerating *spiritual* evolution while carrying out the necessary *earthly* roles. How can we integrate the emotional, physiological, mental, and spiritual aspects of man? At the individual level, this begins with the maintenance of healthy

minds and bodies and the development of personal virtues; at the social level, with the formation of values and their application as ethics in everyday life.

These challenges of the future—and present—are interrelated. They can be seen to reflect many of the problems posed by Plato in *The Republic*; that we have not found the answers to problems posed millennia ago suggests that we will have them with us for some time. This does not mean that they can be ignored. On the contrary, they are among our most important problems, and in preparing for the future we have to give them close and continuing attention.

Although we cannot expect utopia on the basis of our response to these challenges, we can expect in the twenty-first century that some significant shifts will have resulted from the way in which we respond. For example, progress is not likely to be conceived as it is now in a form of continued growth of *material* goods and services. We may still be counting goods and services, but what we characterize as "good" will certainly be significantly different. It is likely that we will be counting non-market goods in a new conceptualization of GNP as "Gross National *Progress*," or even intangibles in a calculation of "Net National Happiness." The first would require us to deduct all expenditures, including health maintenance, which merely keep us where we are; the second requires inclusion of psychic income. A substantial reduction will occur under either calculation in the types of resources used to produce the "goods" desired, permitting a relative shift of material goods to the so-called have-not nations.

Progress in the more advanced nations will be conceived as increased encouragement of each individual to develop in his own unique way, yet without the separateness implied by present-day individualism. Although "basic human needs" will probably have been met, with the concept formulated in terms of quantities, the characterization will include more than material support—such as filial love and place in the community. Greater attention will be paid to those inputs which permit self-actualization of the individual without damage to the society. As a consequence, food consumption will shift towards those items providing greater nutrition to the mind and body. Growth may well be measured by each individual's development—including cultural, intellectual, inquisitive, emotional, and spiritual growth. Such a shift in the concept of growth will significantly alter the way in which we measure our progress.

The greater stress on individual growth will be matched by a greater recognition of interdependence around the world. The experience of the last part of the twentieth century will strongly impress on the peoples of the world the systemic influence of events anywhere in the world. All people are affected by events in any *one* location. A shift is likely to occur in the concept of competition to "win" against others to a "competition of ideas" within cooperative enterprises to achieve a more balanced and equitable growth for the world. Such interdependence will dampen adversarial conflicts, including conflicts between labor and management and leading to the demise of collective bargaining. With more cooperative and less adversarial relations, income distribution will not be a matter of strikes and confrontations, but instead a matter of following acceptable rules within society for matching talents, tasks, and rewards.

Our present inability to achieve such an acceptable procedure is tearing the social fabric and is a major cause of present-day inflation. Society cannot go on in its present form without recognizing that alternate procedures are required to maintain social stability in the twenty-first century. How these decisions are made and concluded will determine both the modes of production and the location of economic activity around the world. It is highly likely that the nations of the world will seek to protect themselves against pressures for rapid adjustment to technological change. At the same time, they will seek to gain advantage from expanded markets through regional integration, which is a necessary step toward worldwide integration.

With the changes described above, equity capital will no longer be seen as the *residual* element in the factors of production in an enterprise and thereby the recipient of the profits. *All* factors will be seen to bear the risk—to the extent that the private sector is risk-bearing in the future. Greater stability of employment (place) will be achieved, with fewer closings of companies, through more flexible use of capital equipment and labor, such as multiple skills training, and therefore more diverse and flexible productive capacity. There will be less waste in investment as a consequence. Profit sharing will occur on a wider scale—if in fact what remains after all factors are rewarded is deemed "profit" by the year 2000. The absence of confrontation among factors will also mean a greater participation in the determination of roles within these producing units—roles which are not likely to mirror what we have today.

With greater cooperation and an assessment of social impact, a reduction of governmental regulation is foreseeable, supported by greater self- and group-discipline. It is only through acceptance of responsibility that the rights of individuals, so often *claimed* in the U.S. today, can in fact be gained.

If we were to look at the place of the U.S. in this system and ask if it will have a leadership role, the answer remains as it has in the past: in a peaceful world, leadership falls to those who have shown how to meet their own problems. Nations seeking to evolve are constantly looking for models of how to maintain unity with diversity, to progress without fouling their own nest, to provide opportunity to all, to meet change without social disruption, and to humanize labor. U.S. models will not be *for export*, but they can be *imported* by those who see them as appropriate. Our task is to deal with the problems we ourselves face, explaining to others how we apply our own values so that they can accept, reject, or adapt the models appropriately.

There appears at present to be increased confidence that the developing countries know best how they should proceed into the twenty-first century, while there seems to be a loss of confidence in the advanced countries. To my mind, this loss of confidence stems directly from the fact that we have placed pursuit of *goods* above pursuit of *"the good."* We have found that mere material growth does not solve our problems or provide individual or social happiness; meanwhile, we have lost our sense of mission. We have substituted measurable material advance for the non-quantifiable aspects of happiness. We have made tradeoffs to maximize output without regard for inputs, especially the drain on the environment, rather than seeking qualitative goals and ways to minimize inputs so as to impose the least burden on the environment. There is nothing wrong with material progress, of course, as long as it is *not* an end itself but subordinate to higher values, and *is* pursued in accordance with these values.

THE NEXT TWO DECADES

Twenty years may seem a short time to prepare for the twenty-first century. It happens to be the same length of time during which the multinational corporation has risen to its current pre-eminence in the world economic scene. We can, therefore, expect comparable change in the international economic order during the next twenty years, in transition to the even more rapid evolution of the twenty-first century. Given certain assumptions, we can paint the transition period with fairly broad strokes. These *assumptions* include a slowing of population growth, no significant weather shifts or natural catastrophes, no significant wars, continued concern with poverty in the Fourth World, and continued technological advancement. On this basis, we can say that five significant shifts are likely to take place in the next twenty years:

1. A new international economic order will be created, forcing considerable changes in the way business is organized and the way it responds to markets. This "order" will not be formed by a worldwide agreement on the rules of the game. It will be an order derived from considerable jockeying and positioning, which leads in turn to shifts in market demands, governmental regulations, technology and innovation, and the organization and role of transnational corporations. The political–economic structure of this order will be based on regional blocs rather than "one world" concepts.

We can already see that for the next two decades the significance of the markets in developing countries will increase considerably. This change will be matched by shifts in the structure of the market, since some of the developing countries will join what are now called the "newly industrialized countries" (NICs), adopting a demand structure more similar to the advanced countries than to the remaining developing countries (LDCs). A strong demand for "basic human needs" will arise in the Fourth World and be met during the next two decades. Governmental demands will be injected in the market in the form of cooperative intergovernmental projects in areas which cannot be met by private demand, such as regional development, space exploration, communication and transportation, and development of ocean resources.

The location of world resources in many LDCs indicates a shift in their processing and final use towards the developing countries, with consequent adjustments in trade patterns, pricing, production and employment in the advanced countries.

Political and economic realignments will alter the setting of international business. Accommodations between Japan and China will be the basis for formation of a bloc in Southeast Asia. The Middle East situation is likely to remain unstable for quite a while, but a bloc will form among Islamic countries of the region. Europe, with Israel and Greece, will form a *loose* economic association with Eastern Europe and Russia (assuming peace, that is, or at least no war; war would cause many realignments). North and South America will begin formation of a bloc, initially only economic. The African countries will form agreements, the substance of which will be slow in developing. These blocs will lead to reformation of the structure and role of the United Nations towards greater concern with interregional affairs.

Science and technology will open up new areas of activity including new energy sources, new techniques for communication which substitute for the physical movement of people, new production techniques which will shift some industries out of developing countries and back into the advanced countries, and wholly new product lines to satisfy consumers' needs and demands.

The role and organization of transnational corporations will also shift as a consequence. In many sectors, there will be increased concentration on a worldwide scale, with a few large companies dominating an industrial sector and having satellite companies in each region. Consortia will be formed on a scale sufficient to meet some of the worldwide problems which require for their resolution massive managerial, technical, and human resources.

2. The criteria for acceptability of the activities of transnational companies and governments will change during the next two decades in the course of developing a new international economic order. The change will reflect a shift in priority from efficiency in production to equity in the distribution of benefits, including the location of production. Greater emphasis on participative decision making in companies and governments will lead to possible conflicts between job security and innovation. Innovation will be favored within fairly stable systems, so change will occur from new combinations of factors and training of labor rather than hiring and firing.

3. As a result of the changes indicated above, industries will relocate their activities around the world, some shifting into developing countries on a sequential basis, following either natural or controlled comparative advantages. Shifting will also occur in the advanced regions on the basis of governmental policies, company structures and objectives, changes in exchange rates, and other factors. These shifts will demonstrate that it is possible to *design* the international economy and that inefficiencies result from conflicting efforts to achieve national benefits; this in turn will lead to greater regional cooperation. It will become clear that we have no criteria for determining the location of industrial activity—that is, who should produce what, where, and sell to whom. The immobility of a production system—once its physical hardware and the accompanying software are in place—plus the increased mobility of individual factors of production will increase the pressure for systems-designed development, including rules for what the system should do and how it should operate. Agreement on the rules will be achieved within regions; rules among regions will apply to only a few types of interactions.

4. All of these shifts will require considerable adjustment on the part of national economies and governments. For example, the increasing significance of agriculture in terms of total world needs will

necessitate the shift of much agricultural production to the U.S., with its comparative advantage in this sector. Although still more sophisticated technology will push the growth of advanced countries still further, they will continue to face the problems of appropriate utilization of labor, increasing attention to leisure, continuing education, and labor training in order to maintain productivity. Efforts to enhance respect for all work within society will raise the perception of equity and thereby raise productivity, as a result of increased personal satisfaction. Adjustments within nations will not be made, however, unless there is also an increasing sense of community among nations, most likely at the regional level. The pressure to match availability of resources to market growth and human needs among several countries will also encourage regionalism.

5. To meet these changes, business managers will need to develop more complex capabilities in dealing with systemic problems. Companies will need to interface with multiple elements of the society in order for their more complex and responsive role to be accepted. The increased concern for "business in the environment," "business in society" and "business ethics" reflects the beginning of a trend. The growing concern of managers for development of personnel with multiple orientations and capabilities is, likewise, a recognition of the complexities of the future. The number of groups with which managers must interact is matched by the varied cultures within which they must operate around the world. At the same time, they must pursue unified corporate objectives under a strategy that is acceptable to all of the communities affected. They must demonstrate that they are taking into account the concerns and objectives of each group involved in a manner which is at least minimally acceptable. Management must use these next twenty years, therefore, to become more attuned to multiple pressures and undertake wider responsibilities.

PREPARATORY STEPS

In making the transition and preparing for the challenges of the twenty-first century, four areas need especial attention. These have to do with education, inequalities of opportunity, the concept of evolution, and the direction of technology.

1. The interdependencies and complexities we face call for a return to holistic instruction. Progressive classification and separation of academic disciplines has virtually run its course, and we need now to reintroduce more systemic approaches to learning and its applica-

tion. The concept of the unity of knowledge has been lost, especially in the realms of science and religion and the conceptual separation of man and his environment. These concepts can and will be reintegrated as we recognize the complexity of relationships.

Greater attention needs to be given to *continuing* education—a departure from the practice of terminating education before the student has a chance to experiment with what he has learned. Experience is still the best teacher for the problems we face, but it would be desirable to provide actual facilities for continued development of new skills, preparation for new roles, and formation of new perceptions of individual, social, and economic progress.

2. Democratic societies have long called for equality of opportunity. If we are to meet the challenges ahead, we will need all of the resources available. We need to make certain that educational and career opportunities are as open as possible, and that the individuals moving into them are adequately prepared—in terms of skills and concepts, as well as an understanding of the rights and responsibilities of individuals. Since the distribution of benefits will necessarily be unequal, as a result of unequal contributions, we will need to design a system of selection, work, and rewards that is understood and acceptable.

3. All individuals need to be better prepared for changes in social and cultural relations. These changes are not dictated by any one person but by global evolution. We need a concept of evolutionary change in individuals and in societies which permits, again, unity with diversity. Too much emphasis has been placed in the past on satisfaction of an individual's material desires and not enough on his *evolution* or that of the society, as a *result* of individual progress and evolution.

4. Technology needs to be increasingly oriented away from military activities; witness the technological advances of Germany and Japan *without* spin-offs of military technology. The orientation should be towards solving the socio-economic problems of urbanization, rural/urban balance, dispersion of industry, agricultural production, health maintenance, new communication modes, less movement of people with greater movement of goods and services—all through technologies which permit the minimization of inputs for desired outputs, rather than the maximization of outputs without regard to non-market costs.

In sum, we need increasing recognition of the fact that we are all in this world together, and that only together can we solve our problems. This requires individual and social evolution exercising greater self-discipline and creativity—a path which does not include our tearing at each other or tearing up our environment, but requires instead that we learn to live with and help each other to evolve toward individual and social perfection.

SELECTED READINGS

Bell, Daniel. *The Coming of Post-Industrial Society.* New York: Basic Books, 1973.

Cleveland, Harlan. *The Future Executive.* New York: Harper & Row, 1972.

Daley, H. E. *Toward a Steady-State Economy.* San Francisco: W. H. Freeman, 1973.

Madden, C. M. *Clash of Culture: Management is an Age of Changing Values.* Washington, D.C.: National Planning Association, 1972.

Mesarovic, N. L., and E. Pestel. *Mankind at the Turning Point.* New York: E. P. Dutton and Co., 1974.

Viola, R. H. *Organizations in a Changing Society.* Philadelphia: W. B. Saunders Co., 1977.

Epilogue

The system we call Capitalism has been the economic paradigm in the Western world for only about 200 years. It has changed significantly during this time and will pass into history, as have all other systems, in due time. Human life itself has lasted for a period of time which is insignificant in comparison to the life of the earth, to say nothing of the universe's estimated twenty billion years. Suppose we were to write the history of the four billion years of the earth's existence in forty volumes, each covering 100 million years in 1000 pages. Each page would encompass 100,000 years; at 1000 words per page, each word would cover 100 years. The dinosaurs would require 5000 pages in the last six volumes, and man would appear somewhere in the last 150 pages of Volume 40, with "homo sapiens" in the last five pages. Western civilization would be recorded in the last fifty-five words, Christianity in the last twenty, and Capitalism would be described in the last two words. Your life story would be contained in the period at the end of the last sentence. What is to be the first word of Volume 41, describing the next 100 years, from 1980 to 2080?

We conduct our lives as though there will be no fundamental change in our society or ourselves. In fact, we are participants in a vast evolution, and not to make progress is to miss the mark and to void the very reason for our being here. Since the process of evolution is so vast, however, it is highly unlikely that an individual's not responding will stop or slow that process significantly. *Time* will march on, changing mind and matter, and hopefully elevating the spirit.

What is going to happen to the economic system and the business system within it? What will be the predominant forces for change? What should the businessman look out for? First and foremost are the changes we discussed in values and the decision systems that will put them into effect. Second, and not far behind, are the new technologies which will be pouring forth as man exercises an increasingly creative mind in an effort to mold or redesign matter to serve his purposes. The technologies that will be available in the twenty-first century are not only mind-boggling (though they will seem merely interesting when we get there); they will also raise acute ethical problems about the proper use of those technologies. We already see these issues reflected in the controversy over genetic engineering. What will we do if we solve the problem of energy? What becomes of man if he solves the problem of producing enough material goods? To what does he turn his imagination and development?

A system not oriented toward increased production of material goods would be radically different from our current system. Since it is conceivable that material growth will not be a problem in the mid-twenty-first century, we should consider such changes in aim. We may still have problems of choice, but scarcity is not likely to be the central problem of decision making.

We are talking about the system of our children and our grandchildren. It will not be Capitalism. Are we preparing for it adequately? Who will be the leaders in that preparation? Will business managers be at the fringes of social change once again? Or will they have gained sufficient perspective of holistic relationships to contribute substantially to the design and construction of the new, total design?

SELECTED READINGS

Callahan, Daniel. *The Tyranny of Survival.* New York: Macmillan, 1973.

Ferleis, V. C. *The Future of Technological Civilization.* New York: Geo. Braziller, 1974.

Hardin, G. *Exploring New Ethics for Survival.* Baltimore: Penguin Books, 1972.

The following journals are also recommended:

Challenge, the Magazine of Economic Affairs
Commentary
Discover
Mother Jones
Next
Psychology Today
Public Policy
Quest
Science
Science 80
Scientific American
The Futurist
The Humanist

Jack N. Behrman is Luther Hodges Distinguished Professor at the University of North Carolina Graduate School of Business Administration, where he is responsible for programs on business roles in society, business ethics, and international business. He has held faculty appointments at Davidson College, Washington and Lee University, and the University of Delaware, and visiting professorships at George Washington University and the Harvard Business School. In addition, Dr. Behrman is a frequent member of research panels for the National Academy of Science and the National Academy of Engineering; an advisor to the U.S. Department of State and the U.N. Centre on Transnational Corporations; and Senior Research Advisor to the Fund for Multinational Management Education in New York. From 1961 to 1964, he was Assistant Secretary of Commerce for Domestic and International Business. Dr. Behrman is the author of numerous articles, books, and monographs, including *Some Patterns in the Rise of the Multinational Enterprise* (1969) *National Interests and the Multinational Enterprise* (1970), *U.S. International Business and Governments* (1971) *The Role of International Companies in Latin American Integration* (1972), and *Industry Ties with Science and Technology Policies in Developing Countries* (1980). In addition, he is coauthor of *International Business-Government Communications* (1975), *Transfers of Manufacturing Technology Within Multinational Enterprises* (1976), *Overseas R&D Activities of Transnational Companies* (1980), and *Science and Technology for Development* (1980).